THE ACTUAL ONE

The

ACTUAL

One

HOW I TRIED, AND FAILED,
TO AVOID ADULTHOOD FOREVER

ISY SUTTIE

HARPER ⬤ PERENNIAL

NEW YORK • LONDON • TORONTO • SYDNEY • NEW DELHI • AUCKLAND

HarperCollins
PUBLISHERS
Since 1817

Originally published in Great Britain in 2016 by Weidenfeld &
Nicolson.

FIRST EDITION

Designed by Jamie Lynn Kerner

Library of Congress Cataloging-in-Publication Data

Names: Suttie, Isy, 1978– author.
Title: The actual one : how I tried, and failed, to avoid adulthood
    forever / Isy Suttie.
Description: First Edition. | New York : HarperPerennial, 2017.
Identifiers: LCCN 2016032314 | ISBN 9780062571977 (trade
    pbk.) | ISBN 9780062571984 (ebook)
Subjects: LCSH: Suttie, Isy, 1978– | Actors—Great Britain—
    Biography. | Comedians—Great Britain—Biography. | Authors,
    English—21st century—Biography. | Adulthood—Humor.
Classification: LCC PN2598.S86 A3 2017 | DDC 791.4302/8092 [B]
    —dc23 LC record available at https://lccn.loc.gov/2016032314

ISBN 978-0-06-257197-7

17 18 19 20 21 LSC 10 9 8 7 6 5 4 3 2

For my dad

THE ACTUAL ONE

1

Isy tries solo skinny-dipping

All right then, I will!" I yelled at Mark, wriggling out of my fleece, T-shirt, two undershirts, bra, jeans, long johns, underwear, leg warmers, socks, and shoes, in that order, tossing them aggressively onto the sand.

"I didn't say anything!" he shouted into the fierce January wind, he and my other two mates looking on bewildered as I sprinted, Day-Glo naked, toward the unforgiving arms of the Celtic sea.

Don't stop running from the bastards, I thought. *No matter how cold it is. Whatever you do, don't stand still.*

Tiny ice-cold fingers jabbed at my everywheres as I took one step, and then another, into the freezing cold water. I tried to run farther in, but my body went limp in protest. I was like a fly in treacle. As I sank down onto my knees instead, my every pore screamed out as I submerged myself up to my neck. I stubbornly faced the horizon for a few seconds, then turned around to look back at them on the shore, positive that their silence was due to their having nicked my clothes and scarpered to a hiding place behind some rocks. Surely that was it. I'd done a crazy thing and they'd nicked my clothes. We were still OK. We were all dicking about. We didn't have to grow up yet.

And I turned, my blood already changing to strawberry Slush Puppie in my veins, and there they were, my three best mates. They weren't hiding behind any rocks, and nobody had hidden my clothes. They weren't even looking my way. Amy was tiredly chucking pebbles at Gavin's foot, Gavin was texting, and Mark was sipping tea from a thermos. I left the sea and made my way back toward them. In the film version of this scene, the woman emerges from the water onto the deserted beach awakened, sexy, rejuvenated, never more alive. In the real-life version, I'd never been more dead. Back I trudged. My thighs were sporting that mottled raspberry-ripple look I'd last exhibited on the netball court at fifteen, my hair was stuck to my face in wet gloops, and my skin was becoming numb. Suddenly painfully aware that they could see everything, I turned round and attempted a sort of backward hop toward them on the sand, showing them just my bum. Good old bums, the same on each sex, neutral—the Switzerland of the anatomy.

I finally reached them, and sulkily yanked my crumpled clothes off the ground and back on as they averted their eyes.

"What did you do that for?" mumbled Mark, screwing the lid back on his thermos. "We'll hit rush hour now."

As we all hurried to the car in silence, it dawned on me that I had reached the point where my mates' hiding my clothes behind a rock was a better scenario than my mates' not hiding my clothes behind a rock. How had it come to this?

REWIND TWO days. It's December 30, and the four of us have stopped at a service station on the way to the beach cottage in Wales for our annual New Year's piss-up. I'd been to the loo and everyone was taking ages, so I was standing aimlessly next to WHSmith doing what I always do at service stations: kicking the floor; checking out travel pillows and thinking how useful they are but how they take up so much room in a suitcase; watching sunburned kids gleefully drizzle Fanta into the creases in those massage chairs. Eventually I entered the shop, lifted a fizzy cola bottle from Pick 'n' Mix as a sweet, sweet micro "screw you" to The Man, swallowed it whole, and then promptly bought a packet of Rolos out of guilt. Amy and Gavin, the only couple I know where I'm friends with both of them equally, scuttled round from the toilet area as I came out of the shop.

"Do you want my first Rolo?" I asked Amy. "That means I hate you."

"Actually I'm feeling a bit *sick*, so I can't," she said. She glanced nervously at Gav.

"You can just bite off the outside," I suggested. "I'll have the toffee. Even though it'll have your germs on it."

This time she ignored me. She looked at Gav again. He grinned now, and the two of them took on a kind of holy sheen. She spoke again. "Isobel Jane Suttie, we've got something to tell you."

The sentence "We've got something to tell you" is the benevolent cousin of "We need to talk." Other relatives include "Are you sitting down?" and "Are you standing up?" and "Are you standing on a bouncy castle?" Everyone knows that "We need to talk" is never, ever good. When you're a teenager, it means that the person who's said it is going to talk for a long time and that the other person is going to sit on a swing with their heart going like a machine gun, using their tatty cuff to wipe away the tears and snot. "We've got something to tell you," on the other hand, is normally about good news for the speakers—the clue's in the plural. "We've got something to tell you" is usually about a matter concerning the speakers rather than you, the audience, unless your doctor likes to hire barbershop quartets to deliver the news of a terminal illness.

"Mmmm hmmm," I said in response to Amy and Gav, feigning nonchalance as I tipped loads of Rolos into my mouth while grasping the nearest thing for support—one of those machines where you operate a metal claw, which I've only ever seen pick up a toy once; it then dropped it again, just before it got to the chute. Don't ever bother with those machines unless you want to teach a child never to trust anyone. I had a bad feeling about whatever Amy and Gavin were going to tell me. They obviously had a very good feeling about whatever they were going to tell me. Beaming from ear to ear, they then proceeded to say one word each. I dread to think how they decided to do this and whether they did it for everyone they were telling. Amy said, "We," Gav said, "Are," Amy said, "Going," Gav said, "To," Amy said, "To," and Gav said, "No, I just said *to*, it's *have* now." They giggled for a few seconds as my knuckles whitened.

"Shall we start again?" said Amy.

"No," I said, "I think I'm getting the—"

Gav interrupted. "Have," he said, "A," Amy chortled, and I said, my mouth a cave of sugary stalactites, "Latte? Fry-up?* Bath?" and they grinned, took a breath, and, in unison, said the word I'd been most expecting, and most dreading. "Baby."

"Oooffft!" I managed. Then, "Well done."

"Awwww," they said. "Auntie Isy."

In fact, that was the first, but not the last, time I heard the term *Auntie Isy. Auntie Isy* drummed up a picture of an old woman in a black dress who's never married, who's covered in cat hair, and who has a permanent trail of cake crumbs across her neglected décolletage. "Auntie Isy? Oh, she had a suitor once. He worked at the Spam factory. That was years ago. Still, she's happy in her way. She has her tapestry." I didn't want to be Auntie Isy, and I sure didn't want them to be Mummy and Daddy. I was aware that I should have been pleased for them, but my heart was plunging deep down into my sneakers, and no amount of Rolos could stop it.

---

* Favored by students and truck drivers but mostly by anyone with a hangover, a fry-up is a massive plate of fried food, often eaten in a café that smells of a thousand bottles of gorgeously burned oil, and which usually includes sausages, eggs, bacon, mushrooms, tomatoes, bread, baked beans, and bubble and squeak (which sounds like a nineties pop duo but is in fact a delicious selection of potatoes, cabbage, and whatever leftovers said café could find—fried, of course). It's the kind of thing that would make Sarah Jessica Parker leave the country, and it's central to British culture, along with queuing and apologizing.

2

An explanation

Let me press pause here, guys, before you think I'm a total bitch. It wasn't that I wasn't pleased that they were so excited. Of course I was. It's just that I didn't know how I'd fit in now. I wasn't a natural with children—the only things that had run through my head the few times I'd been around a very little baby were the same things that had run through my head in school netball lessons: "Don't drop it don't drop it" and "At all costs, avoid the one in the red bib"—but I knew *they* would be. They were two of the best people I'd ever met, and they were going to bring another human being onto this earth! He or she might become—in order of desirability—a humanitarian, a tennis champion, a firefighter, an IT person, a prostitute, an insurance broker. And I would know this kid, and love it (hopefully) as much as I loved them.

It was just such a shock that this was happening now.

These were supposed to be the last few halcyon days before we finally settled down. We were in our mid-to-late twenties, in that wilderness where you stop listening to current music and "rediscover" your favorite band from the nineties—in my case, the seminal punk-cum-indie band Carter the Unstoppable Sex Machine. You buy skinny T-shirts with the band's logo emblazoned on them only to find that they don't fit like they used to, and you plan an expedition to see them play a reunion gig only to find out that your cousin's getting married the same weekend and you've got to do a reading of a poem she's penned herself, which contains lines like "I always threw away the travel section of *The Guardian* till I met you" and "I love the way we use your ex-girlfriend's wineglasses and both feel nothing but jubilation and I genuinely wish her the best." OK, that second line was an exaggeration, but you get the drift. Stuff about chocolate sprinkles on cappuccinos and long Sunday treks and flakes of croissants and sweaty palms being entwined for hours. We were in that wilderness where, if you're unlucky enough to be a member of Facebook, people suddenly and without warning start replacing their profile pictures of themselves drinking from a pineapple in Costa Rica, drunkenly covered in dribble and puke, with a close-up of their baby covered in dribble and puke, wearing a tiny Carter the Unstoppable Sex Machine T-shirt. The one thing worse than the selfie is the selfie by proxy.

We were at the time when the dastardly hat trick of mortgages, marriage, and kids starts to pursue you. It begins with a whiff of it, and you think you're mistaken, but then it's a definite aroma, and before you know it it's like Temple Run and you've got to check over your shoulder for it constantly, and you do daring things to confuse and escape it, like an impromptu trip to Berlin with someone called Chantal you met in Kmart in the early hours, like snorting nutmeg off a trash can, like pretending to be a mystery shopper in order to get free burritos. In my head, my mates and I were going to get married one day at the same time in a massive pagoda on the beach, containing thousands of wedding guests who cheered for "their" couple like at a festival but listened kindly to the support acts they'd never heard of. We'd all get pregnant on the same night (not in the same room, but in the same county), then all live on the same street, and all die on the same day, painlessly yet nobly, holding hands. But we all have these intentions. Before you know it, you're a homeowner and parent, chubbing up on special-offer mature cheddar and £6.99 Rioja (£7.99 on weekend nights!), unable to contain yourself when you spy a good drying rack, and buying people gigantic candles and Audrey Hepburn mouse pads for their birthdays.

I don't begrudge anyone happiness. People can rub noses, rub bark, or rub their genitals on sandpaper in darkened rooms—I don't care, as long as they're ultimately kind, can laugh at themselves, and don't say the phrase "Shall I be Mother?" when they pour tea or gravy. I think it's just that I don't like to feel left out. It harks back to school. Those mottled legs never did serve me well in netball. The feeling of being picked last was so familiar, it was like putting on a pair of trusty old slippers. Possibly it was the slippers that held me back, but you weren't allowed to wear Doc Martens on the court. I always wanted to be one of the gang, so I sought out other weirdos who didn't like netball and who made their own clothes. I shaved the sides of my head when everyone else did. I dyed my hair with henna because that's what Hester from two years above did. And now I had a group of mates who were codependent in the same way: there was an unspoken rule that we were moving forward at the same rate. We were solid. We holidayed very drunkenly in the same hovel of a cottage every New Year's. We made each other do dares all night at festivals, which normally involved speaking in Olde English. We had Mega M&M and Movie Sausage and Mash Marathons.* It wasn't like any of us knew Bez from the Happy Mondays, but I like to think we knew how to have a good time. We were conscious that we were dangerously close to growing up and that, like the cast of *Beverly Hills, 90210* and creepy men from small-town nightclubs, our playing age was about six years younger than our real age. But I thought we had a few more years to do just that—play—before finally getting slurped from the wilderness into the vortex.

I didn't much care for this path toward "growing up," and I spent most of it scrabbling around, trying to make sense of my life. Luckily, being a single writer/performer/Pac-Man aficionado allowed me to scrabble around to my heart's content, because I didn't have to inform a boyfriend of my scrabbling schedule and because you don't really have to grow up in my job. Admittedly, at THAT point, to make ends meet I was also working in a call center for a virtually

---

* I don't like calling them *movies*. We only did it to make a nicer-sounding acronym—MMMMSMM.

bankrupt food-delivery company in a corrugated iron shack with no windows, but that made me feel that my options were even more open. Surely they were open. They had to be. At the very least, someone was going to build a window into the wall. Weren't they?

This is a book about what happened after that pivotal moment at the service station when Amy and Gavin, two of the best housemates I've ever had, told me they were having a baby. It's an ode to the wilderness that comprised the last delicious dregs of my twenties: all its brambles, unexpected ditches, sinister wildlife, clearings with dodgy rope swings, and missing signposts. I stumbled through that wilderness on a quest to have as much fun as possible and also find the crème de la men—someone who would make me deliriously happy yet also not let me get lazy yet also not pull me up on it when I did, thank you very much. If I was ever going to go in for wearing matching underwear and drinking wine from glasses instead of mugs and using oven mitts instead of T-shirts and all that bollocks, I didn't just want The One. I wanted The Actual One.

3

Isy makes a massive penguin

But for now we're in the service station, I'm still reeling from Amy and Gav's pregnancy news, and some poor eight-year-old's sobbing because his dad's now spent six pounds on the claw machine but SpongeBob SquarePants refuses to budge an inch.

"We wanted to tell you now," said Amy, "so you didn't wonder why I wasn't drinking."

Mark emerged from the men's loos, flapping his massive hands from side to side in the air to dry them.

"You know that defeats the point of washing them?" I snapped. "I read it in *Metro*."

He smiled. "You've told her, then?"

"Yeah," said Amy and Gav in unison.

"We didn't know whether to," added Gav, putting his arm round me. "We know it's a hard time for you."

"What with the breakup," Amy added, like in a shit film script.

REWIND TEN days. I'm going out with a guy called Sam, who I've been with for a good few years. For all intents and purposes, he's The One. I know he's The One because it's a Sturdy Relationship™. We really make each other laugh. We both secretly love Queen and openly love *Curb Your Enthusiasm*. He's intelligent (i.e., he wears glasses), he has two good shirts, and he uses a wide vocabulary that includes approximately eighteen words that contain more than five syllables. He shaves often, but we sing along to Randy Newman while he does, so I don't notice how much. He bites the nail of his right thumb only, having pared it down from all his fingers over the years. He wears one pair of Adidas until they're rendered broken, then buys exactly the same pair again, sometimes online if he can't find them in this country. He's compact, personality-wise: holds back for months, then surprises me by getting upset because I've missed our anniversary; and he doesn't shout or cry easily—very British, I suppose. I often feel that not all of him is in the room, like there's a secret bit, and sometimes I think, "No, this *is* all of him." He likes to keep me separate from his friends, on the whole. We live about twenty-five minutes from each other. We have sex about half as much as I say we do when we fill in a magazine survey, the same as every other couple in a long-term relationship. I'd be able to pick out the sound of him breathing in if I closed my eyes and someone got a hundred men to line up and inhale in turn.

Which I'd love to set up, incidentally. Of course, it's not as good as it was at the beginning—but what is? The beginning is like a violent fever, often involving frequent sex, frenetic and giggly or intense and tearful like teenage poetry. As time moves on, the bubble doesn't so much burst as disintegrate, depositing slivers of film over what's really inside.

This year, for the first time, Sam had asked me if I wanted to spend one night at his family's house on December 20, before I went to my parents' house in Matlock for Christmas. What actually happened was that he texted me to say that his mum had said did I want to come for an early Christmas celebration. *Are we five?* I thought. I was surprised that his mum hadn't texted *my* mum the question. On the train there, though, I remembered how his mum made massive Yorkshire puddings the size of the plate, like miniature paddling pools filled with the contents of a roast, and my spirits soared very high, let me tell you. Her Yorkshire pudding plates were like a grown-up version of my pies. I was going through a big pie-making phase at that time. When I say *pie*, I mean I'd get a dessert bowl and line it with bread, butter side up; fill it with the contents of a fry-up (but no tomatoes, as they make the bread soggy); smear a layer of tomato sauce over the whole shebang; then put another piece of bread on top, butter side down, and sort of seal it around the sides by pressing it together. I'd then get a fork and make two holes in the top so it looked like a pie from a nursery rhyme. And sure, it wasn't a pie in the eyes of the law, but if you believe something's a pie, it *is* a pie. Apart from McDonald's apple pies.

No matter how well you know someone's family, they

always have Christmas customs that throw you off balance. The other family carries them out as normal, because they're as ingrained as that stain on the worktop, but to you, as a stranger witnessing them, they seem outlandish or just plain crazy. My family is as bad as anyone else's. Every Christmas morning we have to get out the posh tableware we only use at Christmas and check all of it for rogue vegetables before we start cooking. This is due to the fact that one year, we were about to place the carrots in a lidded serving dish when we found that lurking in the corner of said dish was a shriveled brussels sprout from exactly a year before. It was brown and tiny and apologetic, like it had retreated in shame. Everyone blamed everyone else, including the sprout itself, but eventually my dad was given the mournful task of chiseling it off with a chopstick and lobbing it into next door's garden—there was an ongoing conflict about a tree. I've always wondered if it grew into a sprout bush, but I've never seen anything that resembles one, as much as I crick my neck peering over the fence.

The other main custom my family has at Christmas is reading aloud other families' round-robin letters—you know, the letters that give a summary of what's happened that year. I find them fascinating reading, not so much because of the facts in them but the way they're written, and why they've chosen to spend a paragraph describing a rainy trip to Yorkshire Sculpture Park with only a brief mention of their daughter's wedding as an addendum.

Every year my mum threatens to write one for our family, and this year she'd e-mailed one round—just to us lot, of course:

Overall, it hasn't been a bad year for the Sutties. Unfortunately, my husband had a bad stub to the toe in March and had to sit down for ten minutes. However, he's been on the mend since, and we're hoping to have him back to his jolly self in time for Christmas Day. Sadly, I haven't been without my fair share of health problems, either. A bad cold in August of all times left me unable to bell-ring one evening, and as a result, people said it didn't sound quite as melodious as usual. We had some new kitchen worktops done in October and no one noticed, so we've started pointing them out aggressively to anyone who comes round. My two daughters remain fine, despite both being unmarried and childless!

When I got to Sam's family's in Croydon, I handed out my mum's round-robin, which I'd printed out, as a kind of early Christmas present. They laughed, because they were great, but I noticed his mum then trying to hide what turned out to be *their* round-robin—and it was a proper one.

"Oh, come on, let me read it!" I said. "My mum only wrote that one to take the piss because nothing goes on in our family."

Eventually they acquiesced, but I soon saw why they'd been reticent about me reading it. It wasn't because they were hurt about the Suttie one; it was because Sam's parents' round-robin mentioned all their kids' boyfriends and girlfriends except me. No wonder—I never saw his parents, lovely as they were.

Reading that round-robin made it clear to me that no matter how much I tried to kid myself, we weren't really considered a couple. His parents hadn't excluded me out of malice—it just hadn't occurred to them. I could have won an Olympic medal, or broken a world record for watching back-to-back episodes of ITV's seminal fantasy gaming show *Knightmare* (ah, another unfulfilled ambition—*Knightmare*, not the Olympics), but it just wouldn't have crossed their minds to mention me. I texted Amy:

> Bloody hell. Sam's parents didn't include me in Xmas round-robin and mentioned all other partners of their kids. Sam's dad just told Sam to take me to the park and he said no, I'm watching football! He can be such a twat x.

And then the inevitable happened. I sent the text to Sam's phone. I always thought it was an urban myth that you could send a text to the person the text was about, but I'd just actually done it. What's more, I'd done it about a delicate matter. No matter how annoyed I was, I couldn't deal with the idea that things maybe weren't going quite as well as Sam and I were both pretending they were. I was appalled at the idea of his knowing how hurt I was about the round-robin and then his telling his mum and the subsequent shitstorm stalling the arrival of the giant Yorkshire puddings. I had to get to that phone and delete it.

Sam's phone—an old Nokia with an actual antenna like a child had designed it—was in the pocket of his black fleece jacket, which was hanging in a closet that everyone could see. I couldn't just go and get it without explaining myself. The house was pretty hot. The only thing I could think of to do was to pretend to be cold. I tried chattering my teeth but realized that's only done in cartoons. I rubbed my bare arms. Yes, this felt convincing.

"'Ooh, I'm freezing!" I said lightly to him. "Can I have your fleece?"

"Have this," his mum said kindly, taking a crocheted blanket from the arm of the settee.

"The thing is," I replied, "when I'm cold I really need something covering the whole of my arms. I often sleep in a tracksuit in bed."

What was this? I was going totally off piste. A tracksuit? Why didn't I just say *pajamas*? Maybe I'd make an appearance in next year's round-robin whether I liked it or not.

"Do you want a cup of tea?" his dad said, getting up. "Tea warms you up when you're cold and cools you down when you're warm! Ah, tea!"

"No, I just really want Sam's fleece!" I almost shouted, then added, "It smells of him."

"Ah!" said his dad. "Not tea! Fleece!"

There was silence.

"Go and get your fleece, then, Sam," his dad said. "You wouldn't take her to the park—this is the least you can do."

Thankfully, Sam was playing a game of Operation with his brother that had twenty quid riding on it.

"Don't worry," I shouted, running toward the closet, "I'll get it. Wouldn't want you to drop that kidney."

I got it and put it on, zipping it up as I felt I should, while furtively feeling in the pocket for the chunky phone. There it was, heavy in my hand like the gorgeous brick it was. I sat back on the sofa for a few moments, utterly boiling but giddily triumphant. But how was I going to do this? I couldn't get his phone out then and there. Then I remembered: I could go to the loo. The good old loo. Safe in the confines of freshly laundered towels and a carefully locked door, I deleted the text at last. I also took the opportunity to see who else had been texting him. Maybe he was having a secret affair. It was all people I knew—his mates. I was almost disappointed.

Later that night, after I'd opened Sam's gift to me of a Frank Zappa T-shirt plus a slate chopping board, his mum asked him what I'd gotten for him for Christmas. He looked blank. I couldn't believe it.

"Um . . ." He looked at me searchingly. "*Freaks and Geeks* box set?"

"Yeah," I said, "what was it in?"

He looked at me again. "A case?"

I turned to his mum. "It was in a penguin's stomach," I said.

She looked blank, her forkful of giant Yorkshire pudding wavering between plate and mouth. I smiled and tipped back in my chair. "Yup. I made your son a penguin."

REWIND FIVE days.

I called the penguin Roy because Sam and I had recently been to the London Zoo, and there was a penguin there called Roy whom we fell in love with immediately and couldn't tear ourselves away from. One of Roy's legs was a bit shorter than the other and he was always looking around daydreaming when fish were being handed out, and then he'd try to catch up with the big group of penguins but he couldn't.

I had no idea how to go about making a penguin from scratch, but I knew I wanted him to be big—and sturdy, unlike his real-life counterpart—so I bought a roll of chicken wire that was a good four feet high from the DIY shop, and just bent it round, like the squat body of a snowman. It stayed in that shape, which gave me confidence: the body was complete. I then went to the newsagent downstairs, who gave me a load of out-of-date newspapers, and I slathered papier-mâché all over Roy's body, leaving a vertical opening about a foot wide down his front, like he'd been unzipped. I considered trying to make penguin organs out of papier-mâché and placing them in there, actually a bit like a massive version of Operation, but decided that might be a step too far. I instead constructed "shelves" inside Roy's stomach, made from mesh, which I then also papier-mâchéd. Sam could put DVDs or books inside him. At the top of his body there was a groove for his head, which I made from a bubble lampshade I stole from my living room, stuffed with more newspaper to make it into a ball. His wings were fully rotational, made from a wire frame in a big petal shape with black felt stretched over it, and once they were attached, I painted the whole thing with black gloss paint. An orange papier-mâché beak and painted-on eyes permanently looking left completed him. I realized as I applied the finishing touches that he didn't have feet, but I didn't think that mattered in the grand scheme of things.

Like if you met a mermaid, you'd be so bowled over that you wouldn't notice if she had hairy armpits. Or maybe you would, and you'd like it. I certainly would.

By chance, the newspapers that were stuffed into Roy's head were primarily *The Sun*, which meant that had Roy come to life, he would have had some pretty interesting opinions about other penguins coming over to the UK, and whether it was OK to look at other penguins sunbathing. I was going to write *topless*, but penguins are always topless. As are all other animals, come to think of it. And bottomless. Bloody tarts. Roy's head was great because, as it was totally detachable from his body, he could appear to be in all different kinds of moods—pensive, happy, suicidal—and he could also peer at you with his head on one side, or seemingly out of the corner of his eye, if you stood to his right. There was even the rogue option of his head coming completely off and being positioned under the crook of his wing, like a penguin ghost from a picture book.

Roy was never meant to be some kind of kooky gift. I just like acting on instinct and following things through thoroughly. Roy happened to be born out of a truly spontaneous moment at the zoo. The materials were what they were because I have the three-dimensional art skills of a child. Also, I really adored making him. It was a secret project that started small. By the time I painted the final touch of gloss paint on his beak, I felt a bond with him that no one could break.

As it turns out, if you decide to make a papier-mâché penguin for your partner to try to save your relationship, the raw materials will cost approximately £180 and the reaction will be vague.

I took Roy round to Sam's in mid-December, while we were still in London. I'd been building up this present a lot, and I was confident he would be a hit. As he and I stood on Sam's doorstep after I'd rung the bell—I'd tried to get Roy to do it with his wing, but Sam's neighbor was watching from the bus stop and I felt that it was too much—I said, "OK, buddy, you need to work your magic." Roy looked at me dubiously, with his head on one side. I straightened it. That was better. Wow, I had total control of his emotions, like when you have kids! Sam was opening the door. I had my arm round Roy, who, at five feet, was almost my height. The bus driver had feebly tried to charge me for him, but the rest of the passengers had protested so much when I told them my story that he'd let Roy on for free, and then a few stragglers had clustered round me for the journey, asking how long it took to make Roy and other technical questions like "Is it a panda?" and "Why have you done this?"

The door was fully open now, and Sam stood on the doorstep. His gaze was locked onto my face in the same way men's gazes are when they're trying not to acknowledge the existence of your breasts. Except in this case he was avoiding acknowledgment of the five-foot penguin by my side.

"Hi, Sam," I said. "This is Roy."

He finally took Roy in, like a toddler takes in its newborn sibling and realizes that life will never be quite as simple again.

"Um, hi, Roy," he muttered.

I replied in a high, squeaky voice, "Hello, Sam." What was I doing? Roy wouldn't talk like that. This was all wrong. I decided never to try to speak for Roy again, never to adjust his head. He was a penguin in his own right.

"Is Roy for me?" Sam asked, shooting a glance up and down the street, shiftily waving at the neighbor, who was now watching the show.

"Yup!" I said. We had to get him up the stairs to Sam's flat. He was pretty heavy, especially as I'd packed box sets into his stomach, so we left his head on the doorstep for the first trip, and then I raced back down the stairs to get it. The neighbor, incidentally, had gotten on his bus.

4

Isy cries into bosom of
nameless girl in glittery top

The girl from school whose name I always forget put her arm round me and wiped the mascara from my eyes.

"I made him a fucking penguin for Christmas and he didn't even remember!" I sobbed. "I only gave it to him ten days ago! What would have done it? An elephant? A time machine?"

Another woman pounded on the door and yelled that she needed a wee as I hunkered down on the lid of the toilet, wedged my heels against the door, and sank deeper into the-girl-whose-name-I-always-forget's trusty old bosom, tears staining her sparkly top. What a great Christmas Eve.

I normally loved going back to Matlock at Christmas. Matlock has endless beautiful cliffs, rivers, caves, views, and people, and, like most touristy towns in this country, it also harbors faintly threatening gaggles of piss-bored, pus-ridden, bus-shelter-dwelling, iron-deficient, tatty-cuffed, gaze-dodging, nougat-stealing, cider-swigging, grease-befouled, ne'er-do-wash teenagers who give impromptu renditions of Rage Against the Machine in the park to scare mini-golfers and supply tourists with vague directions to Riber Castle in exchange for Marlboro Reds. I loved those teenagers, too, because I became one at the age of twelve, as was the rule. You can play your child *Peter and the Wolf* all you like when she's in the womb, but you can't stop her cutting Girl Scouts to jump off a bridge into a river for a one-pound bet, breaking her ankle and her mother's heart.*

Each Christmas, everyone from school went out to the Boat House pub like we used to when we were fourteen, and I'd be re-united with people I'd been to gigs with to see Carter and Jesus Jones and the Levellers, and it would feel like no time had passed. Everyone would drink loads and have little joshing arguments about things like "He was in the year above us," "No, he was in our year." There would be people who were now, say, doctors, utterly hammered, clinging to the pinball machine like they were on a sinking ship, shouting, "I told someone they had lupus today! I've just shagged Tim in the bogs! His dick had that knobbly bit at the end, like it said on that desk in 1992! He wouldn't let me give my professional opinion on it!" Truces would be made between sworn nineties enemies over a shot of vodka, old romances would rekindle, old feuds would resurface. It was the best place to be if you were from Matlock and graduated from Highfields between 1998 and 2001, and the worst place to be if you were from anywhere else in the world. It's the same the country over.

---

*To get out of my exams, I accepted a challenge to jump off the bridge in Matlock Park for a pound. It was raining, and the water looked deeper than it was. I landed with my foot at a right angle to my ankle. All my friends promptly scarpered except for Erin Condron, who found a fiver on the ground and went to buy a pack of Marlboro Reds but came back for me, and sourced the skateboard that I would be wheeled home on.

This year, though, the drunker I got, the more I knew that Sam and I were kaput. Who was I kidding? Sure, it was a Sturdy Relationship™, but it was the kind that was perpetually "nearly there." I constantly felt that if one of us just did one more little thing, everything would fall into place. It was always a case of "He needs more time, then he'll see that we should move in together, rather than buy houses next door to each other, have kids, and let them run through tunnels we've made under our respective houses," like he once suggested.

"It'll be great if one of us runs out of coffee—we'll just go next door!" he'd say, eyes shining, wondering what my problem was. When you didn't need stuff from him, that's when you got it. When you asked him for something, he floundered. He'd stay up all night helping me learn a speech for a casting the next day that I was nervous about but hadn't asked for his help with, making pots of tea and rounds of reassuring toast, but when I really wanted him to come to Leamington Spa for my sister's birthday—an epic "sausage crawl" was planned, where we'd visit all the cafés—he couldn't possibly make it. The sausage crawl was great, by the way. My advice is to pace yourself by opting for a few halves of sausage along the way.

We still slept entwined like we did at the start, but entirely alone, dreaming of our old identities, before the popcorn and the pasta and the obligatory sex. There are a few things that lead to obligatory sex in a long-term relationship. These include: a lunch where items have been bought from the supermarket deli counter; a day on holiday in Spain where you drink too much rosé at dinner and both work to deftly avoid an argument about how far away a castle is; a homemade gift of any kind if they cry as they give it to you, but not including mixtapes or mix-CDs, which are the TV dinners of the homemade gift.

When people asked me how things *were* with Sam (why do people do that? They don't do it to married couples. It's a veiled "Why aren't you married yet?") I'd grin in a sort of lopsided way and say, "Oh, we're muddling along." Unfortunately that would often elicit further questions, so I started to try something my mum does when she doesn't want to answer a question. My mum hates small talk and would much rather discuss how exactly radiators work with a stranger than what she did last week with a friend. So whenever someone asks her, say, "How are your daffodils coming along?" or "How are the girls?" she locks eyes with that person, smiles widely, and says, "Yeeeeeeeeeeeees." Very slowly and pointedly, the word *yes*, but over about five seconds. And they probably think she's misheard, or that something awful's happened to the daffodils, or us, that has so traumatized her that she's just saying "yes," and they never ask again. What a woman! Sadly, it didn't work the same with me—my mates would just go, "Why are you saying *yeeeees*? What's happened now? Let's go for a curry and you can tell me," and then of course I'd say "yes" and mean it, because if there's one thing I've got a penchant for, it's dal and drama in a public place.

Christmas Day was the club sandwich it always is: thin layers of pleasure, primarily due to food or excitement about what to watch on TV, interspersed with rich slabs of ennui and bickering. I wouldn't have it any other way. This time, though, I was troubled. On Boxing Day, I called Sam in Croydon on his shit phone with the stupid antenna and was crying before he even answered. I'd made my decision in the loos with the girl from school on Christmas Eve, but it didn't seem right to break up with someone on Christmas Day. When it came to it, Boxing Day felt pretty wrong, too, like eating chips in a Chinese restaurant. It all tumbled out in fits and starts, jazzlike: bits where I spoke so fast he had to ask me to repeat myself, and sections where there were long silences broken by our irregular sniffs. To my surprise, (a) he agreed with me that things had been going badly and I think he would have ended it himself a few days later, (b) he was upset and actually cried, and (c) he still didn't agree that his nonattendance of the sausage crawl had been a tipping point.

There was no denying that it was finito. Our telltale habit of bantering our way through every situation was conspicuously absent, which told me that there was no hollow plan to "try to make it work," thank God. We didn't pretend we'd try to be friends, even though he was wonderful company and a very kind person. How funny, that you would be able to recognize someone breathing in anywhere, and then with a few words you never see him again.

"I can't come to the cottage for New Year's now," he said. "I'll have to stay at home and break the news to Roy."

That was when he cried. Sam, not Roy. I'm not that fucking good at making penguins.

"WHEN'S SAM dropping round the memory box?" asked Amy jauntily. "We'll be able to watch *Die Hard 2* again when we get it back."

We were out of the service station and back in Keith—Mark's Citroën—driving toward the cottage. I was, I suppose you could say, suffocating my sorrows in Haribo.

"In a few days," I mumbled through luminous additives. Sam was going to drop off the stuff I'd accumulated at his house when I got back from New Year's. On the phone when we'd broken up, he'd referred to this collection of my things as a "memory box." I was going to hand over anything I had of his, and then if I found anything else after he'd gone, I was going to post it to him in a Jiffy bag rather than meeting up for a second time. It was definitely going to be a used Jiffy bag. I wasn't going to go buy a new Jiffy bag for him.

"Is *memory box* a term he's made up," asked Mark, "or some patented thing?"

"I dunno," I muttered, biting the head off a giant yellow jelly snake. "I dunno what's worse."

I thought of poor old Roy the penguin, who used to stare at us every night from the corner of Sam's room with his head on one side and his beady eyes gleaming softly in the moonlight, as if pleading, "I should never have been born." How was Roy going to fit into this bloody memory box?

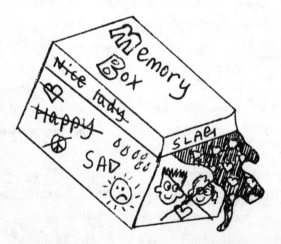

5

Isy meets fake monk

As we got close to the cottage later in the afternoon, I started to cheer up as I saw the lush green hedges whizzing by and breathed in the manure-y smell that heralds local ales and stilted exchanges about hedges with hikers. We traveled down a lane with no discernible name, past rows of tumbling-down barns and orchards with sun-shriveled farmers who stopped raking and stared at Keith the Car like he was a spaceship while Mark waved at them incessantly from the driver's seat. Mark is one of those long-legged, wiry people who wears shorts in November and gets twitchy if he doesn't go outside every couple of hours. He favors his dad's threadbare cardigans and is endlessly capable, especially with electronics and clapped-out VHS recorders. Amy and Gav have been together for years. Amy has an uncanny knack of sensing when people need emotional help, and is drunk the rest of the time—although of course now that she was pregnant, we were all to see behind the magician's cloth. Gav can't be trusted with anything but completely forgets what you've told him the minute after you tell him, so he can't tell anyone, anyway. He's like a parable that can't quite get it together. The cottage is in St. Davids, a great area of Wales, and it's not a holiday cottage, it's a tumbling-down cottage that belongs to Mark's family, so we can spill barbecue sauce on the wallpaper and write "Jizz lords rule OK" in the visitors' book without having to worry about losing our deposit.

Even though we came here every year, we never quite remembered the route. Every lane looked the same. The dog-eared instructions written by Mark's uncle said things like, "Turn left by the cow—she never moves!!!!!" and "Eggs available from Maureen at Croft Farm—leave 50p or equivalent on ledge." What was the equivalent of 50p? Two toffees? A quarter of a sausage? There's a place like that near my parents' in Matlock. You leave the 50p and take the eggs, or a washing machine. We finally reached the cottage. On parking, we saw that there was a bottle of milk on the ground next to the wall, presumably dispensed by the stationary cow, and as the familiar old door creaked open I felt a wash of calm come over me. The cottage was higgledy-piggledy and dusty, and the decor would have been just ahead of its time in the seventies. It was brilliant. And we were on holiday. It was New Year's. Anything could happen—I might meet a local lad and never come home, like when people go on a gap year to Australia and start off working in a bar and next thing, they're married to someone called Brad and they know what boysenberries are.

We slung our bags upstairs—each year we slept all together in a long shadowy room like a dormitory, full of damp and bunk beds—and opened some beers. There was another bedroom on the ground floor, but no one ever slept in it because the mattress was so old. Besides, it was good to all be in the same room. Like Girl Scouts, with booze. Like Girl Scouts, then.

That night we had a roast, then went off to a pub we'd not been to before.

"It's just a short walk, along the north of the coastline," said Mark. It took us forty minutes.

I never understand when people say "to the north of . . ." or even worse, "to the northwest of . . ." Sometime around the age of twenty-five, people in my peer group started celebrating their birthdays by having picnics in parks instead of drunken nights out. I'm guilty of it, too—it seems to be a rite of passage. Bunches of grinning, skinny hipsters turn up clutching bags of Doritos and homemade guacamole they will fight over tooth and nail should someone do a spot of rogue dipping. Girls with flicky black liquid eyeliner glide about in nice flared fifties dresses they haven't quite thought through; they have to adopt all manner of kneeling positions. Someone wispy called Barney or similar brings a kite that lurks on its own away from the food, in its cellophane wrapper, then gets forgotten. Someone brings a dog, or some juggling balls, or a guitar, or a poem. Someone spends the whole time taking photos—making people awkwardly reenact the joint dipping of pita into hummus, their jaw muscles spasming as they try to hold the smile while someone takes the camera phone off night mode—and putting the photos on Twitter and Facebook, then becoming depressed when no one comments on them. I suggest Truth or Dare and everyone smiles and looks into the middle distance. Some plucky dude plays the opening bars to "Here Comes the Sun" and everyone feels a little bit of themselves die inside. Everyone says, "We should do this more!" Anyway, in all the invites to these parties, it says things like, "Meet at the northwest of the fountain." How does anyone know where that is?

The local pub was exactly as it should have been—low beams; dying fire; unsmiling barman; locals with eyes afizz with curiosity and scarcely concealed malice. I always like my holiday pubs to be like something out of *The Wicker Man*. As we approached the bar, pulling our painfully new fleeces over our heads, I had the familiar urge to try to change my accent from English to anything else in the world, or to just point silently at the things I wanted and take my luck. Anything but risk their thinking, wrongly, that we were "those twats." The kind of people who would eventually move here, snapping up locals' houses, with dreams of setting up a writers' retreat or an antique shop; in time, complaining that the village shop closed at five and that Latin wasn't on the primary-school curriculum. It was too late, though. Mark had started ordering a round, in his slightly posh voice. Everything went a bit quiet as you could see all the locals trying to work out which drinks were for Mark and Gavin and which were for me and Amy. I couldn't work it out, either. Mark had ordered two alcoholic drinks and two orange juices. Obviously one juice was for Amy, but what about the other? Gav took it off the bar, grinning.

"Ah yeah, the cat's out of the bag," he said.

What cat, in what bag? Surely he wasn't pregnant as well? I couldn't take much more big news today.

"I'm not drinking. I'm training for an eighth marathon."

As far as I knew, the most Gav had ever run was to get cigarettes and white bread from the newsagent downstairs. Mark and I looked on, astonished.

"Did you say your eighth marathon?" I asked, genuinely impressed. "When did you do the other seven?"

"Erm, no, it's like a marathon," he mumbled. "I'm doing an eighth of it. An eighth marathon. Like, half of a quarter marathon."

"Wow!" I said. "Well done. When is it?"

"March," he said. "But I'm going to be dressed as a chicken, so I need to start training early, to cope with all the extra sweat."

"Just dress as yourself, then," I said.

"Nah," he answered, "I don't want anyone to recognize me if I come last."

What the hell was happening? Amy pregnant, now Gavin starting running. I was newly single, still reeling, and I wanted mates to go out drinking with more than ever. All I needed now was for Mark to announce his plans to become a priest.

Maybe I'd found a new friend, though, in the shape of a man dressed as a monk sitting at the bar. By "dressed as a monk," I mean that he was in no way a monk, although I suppose all monks are men "dressed as monks," just a bit more convincingly than this. This monk was, as my dad would say,

a "character." You could see this in his limbs, before he even
turned his head. You could also tell from the bald cap he was
wearing, which was encircled with black woolen hair. Mark
had ordered a rosé for himself, which had led to much jollity
among the monk and his comrades. The monk then immediately came and sat with us and quizzed us on where we were
from and what we were doing there. At that time, instead of
"cheers," Amy, Gav, Mark, and I used to say, "Ahoy, regards."
This was because we'd recently spent a night pretending to
be polite pirates, and the saying had stuck. We said it to each
other automatically as we clinked drinks, the monk quite
rightly queried it, and we taught it to the monk, who taught
it to the pub, and that tiny moment led to our having one of
the best nights ever. There was a lock-in with us and a few
locals. No one took any photos, even though at one point we
were praying on the floor, with the monk delivering a sermon.
Back at the cottage, Amy went to bed, and Mark, Gav, and I sat
up drinking Baileys and port mixed together, at my behest.
We'd succeeded in persuading Gavin not to dress as a chicken
at the eighth marathon but just to wear his Arsenal outfit with
a Hannibal Lecter mask to conceal his identity, which meant
he could relax his no-drinking rule for a bit, thank God. We'd
gone from two down back to one down.

The next day was New Year's Eve, which always carries that
horrible pressure to have fun. I've been to so many New Year's
house parties filled with a sense of panic—looking around the
room, thinking, *Shit, this is it! At nine o'clock anything seemed
possible, but an hour on, these complete strangers are the people I'm
going to be bringing in the New Year with*—he's *said the word* ran-

dom *twenty-eight times,* she's *virtually asleep, I bet* he *thinks it's* "Old *Lang Syne." I've just got to make the best of this.* It's like that moment just before the final slow song at a nightclub, wishing the lights were better so you could see everyone's shoes, when you drunkenly gravitate toward someone: an eye-level shoulder's an eye-level shoulder, right? You may be able to tell when I stopped going to nightclubs—I'm not sure they play slow songs anymore, and I'm not sure people call them nightclubs anymore. I love the French word for nightclub, *boîte de nuit,* which translates as "night box." I've had many an empty night box on New Year's Eve, let me tell you, and on any normal night I wouldn't have noticed, but most of us want to feel sexually validated on New Year's Eve.

THE NIGHT box was firmly locked and bolted this time. There were no eligible males in this cottage, and I wasn't about to go down the lane, scrabbling among the wheat in search of some D. H. Lawrence-style farmer's son, all ruddy cheeks and dungarees and stuttered monosyllables and muddy palms. "Oive never bin in the haystack apart frem to get rakes. Mind keepin' an eye on Bessie whoile we do it? She's fair ready to drop." I didn't care about any of that tonight. Never open the night box until they've passed the security tests. Never go out without locking it, but also never forget the key. The night box situation was not a problem. We had copious amounts of booze that we were going to make into punch, plus Pop Rocks and raw chili peppers for Amy to replace the booze. What could go wrong?

6

Isy starts a conga that looks like Snake on an old Nokia

We started off New Year's Eve with yet another roast—in the same way that people always cook too much spaghetti, we never cooked quite enough chicken—and then we went on a massive walk with Mark's dog. I haven't mentioned the dog yet because I am really scared of dogs. I don't think there was some terrible childhood incident that led to this, I think it's bloody common sense, because dogs have teeth, no moral code, and an indiscriminate appetite for destruction—toilet-paper rolls, armchairs, humans, they don't give a shit. Even little dogs, which are more like animated teddy bears, make me nervous.

Yet people are so affectionate with their dogs. If I was hugging a mate and she suddenly did a really loud bark in my ear—guess what? I would jump and let go. If I was kissing a bloke and he said, "Oh, by the way, I've just been licking my arms and my bum," I'd be incredibly impressed that he could lick his own bum, so that would override my disgust. But when a dog licks its own bum, that's not an achievement! That's like us moving a vase or closing a briefcase. When a dog refrains from licking its own bum, *that's* something. That's like a human getting out of a tent for a wee when they're zipped into a snuggly sleeping bag. It takes a bit of grit to do that. I respect dogs who *don't* lick their bums. I respect them, but I still abhor them. And anyone who kisses their own dog on the mouth: if you ever, ever come near my night box, prepare to be annihilated. Even if you know all the words to "Ice Ice Baby" backward. No way. Get a life. I do love the way dogs shake themselves dry after they've been swimming, though. If I met someone who dried themselves like that after a shower, it'd be pretty cool. I hate drying myself after a shower. It's a complete waste of time. My skin will eventually dry anyway, so what's the point of rubbing it dry? Talk about trying to get a bloody pot to boil.

Mark's dog is called Moomoo. There's some story about Moomoo's real name, Martin, having been changed because it was too similar to next door's dog's name, although I can't understand the problem with that, unless they looked completely identical and got out of taking walks by sending the other one, their disgusting plan only being unearthed when one trotted in to its master with *The Times* rather than *The Telegraph* in its mouth. Moomoo had never really accepted his new name, hence the trillion (increasing in volume) screams of, "Moomoo, Moomoo, MOOMOO! DOG! DOG! YOU! YES, YOU! BLOODY STOPPPPPPP!" as he ran amok in parks and streets alike. Everyone else in the cottage loved dogs. I think a love or detestation of dogs is innate—like how some people can roll their tongues and their letter *R*s. I can do both of those, *and* I can put out thirteen matches in my mouth. I had to teach myself how to do that, though. I couldn't teach myself to love Moomoo.

It's not that I hate all animals. I love rabbits—although my first pet wasn't one, much to my chagrin. My mum thought my sister and I should "practice" looking after a rabbit by getting a hamster, as if size is directly proportional to amount of care and love required. We got the hamster from the pet shop, and the man seemed really eager to get rid of it. That should have been a warning sign. We called the hamster Paul, and we insisted that Paul was an "it." Everything was genderless then, in the halcyon days. Good job we didn't live in France. My sister and I took Paul home and dreamed of teaching it tricks, of its winning prizes, of its scrapping with next door's dog and winning.

One morning, a few weeks later, we came downstairs to discover that Paul had given birth to nine babies in the night. They were all bald and light pink and blind, and squirming around like hell. We watched in disbelief as Paul nonchalantly picked up one that had no arms and legs, and ate it. That morning my mum, my sister, and I marched through the park with the cage held aloft, and back to the pet shop. We had eight baby hamsters and no idea how to care for them. Surely the owner would take them back from us? The owner looked cross and said he might recall selling us Paul, but he couldn't possibly take these babies back into the pet shop. There was a snake in there, for God's sake! It was our fault for being drawn to a pregnant hamster, and we just had to live with the consequences.

As soon as we got home, the three of us cleared out all the drawers in the sideboard and lined them with straw and newspaper. Over the next few weeks, the babies—which were all still in the cage—grew bigger, and then it was time. We put each baby in a drawer of its own, like they were living in a block of flats. By this time we'd named them all, and we made little paper signs that we stuck on each drawer. My sister and I had named four each. My sister's signs said things like, "Mr. Sunshine. Please knock quietly!" I loved the band the Doors, so my signs said things like, "LA Woman. Don't knock. I hate you almost as much as I hate myself." We closed each drawer, leaving a tiny gap for air, and then my sister and I sat down to watch *Gladiators*.* I had just hit fourteen and had such a vicious crush on Hunter that he'd bring on early ovulation whenever he came onscreen. I was in the middle of a daydream about Hunter pursuing me up The Wall when my sister said that we should go check on the hamsters.

When we did so, we found that all of them had climbed out of their respective drawers and were loose around the house. Employing Columbo-like skills, my mum examined the carpet and discovered a trail of droppings that led behind the gas fireplace. We immediately replaced that trail with a trail of lettuce and seeds leading back to the apartments in

---

*A dramatic fitness competition show on TV where, say, a housewife who'd never left Scotland raced through a foam obstacle course against a very pretty, fully trained athlete called something like Doom or Annihilator.

the hope that that evening, they'd blindly follow it and know to climb up into their own drawers. In the morning the food was gone, but we never saw or heard from any of them again. Not even a postcard. We left food out near the gas fireplace every night, and at first it always disappeared, but after a few nights it started to remain there and Dad said we had to accept that they were gone and stop laying out food or we'd get mice. "Brilliant!" we enthused. "Free hamsters!" But it was not to be. We threw away the newspaper and everything else from the drawers, but the apartment signs were stuck fast, and even now, files of bank details and life insurance plans are in drawers on which if you look closely, you can just about make out, on very faded rectangles of yellowing paper, "Mrs. Beady-eyes. I love munching!" and "Riders on the Storm. Get out of my room."

AMY, GAV, Mark, and I set off on the walk with Moomoo, meandering down to the bottom of the garden, through a secret little creaky gate, and into some woods. This was infinitely better than the beach. There's something a bit smug about the sea. It thinks it's full of hidden depths, like some yoga teachers and people who keep their festival wristbands on all year round, but ultimately it's the same through and through— it's loads of salty water. Sure, there are luminous fish and shipwrecks and stuff, but the sea thinks those things owe it a living. They don't. Those things exist independently of the sea, in books and museums and aquariums. Woods are far more romantic to me. With woods, there's always genuine hidden stuff, the jewels of my teenage escapades into dank, mushroomy forest caves: saucepans, love letters, unexplained lengths of white cotton laid down symmetrically, pages ripped from exam prep books, empty Fanta cans, a single running shoe. And here we were in the woods. A roast; a walk with a dog. These were two pretty grown-up things that, say, a fifty-two-year-old couple in Berkshire might do at New Year's, but we'd put our own spin on them. The roast had been overcooked, which had decreased the taste but increased the sense of haphazardness and chutzpah, and the dog was unhinged, so anything could happen. I still had my pajamas on—I'd just put a hoodie and some boots on top. Plus, before causing mayhem in the pub again that night, we were going to make a punch containing a portion of tequila worm each.

That night we got stuck into the punch early, as a starter. Absinthe, Advocaat—all the As—then good old Coca-Cola, gin, and vodka. We didn't put the tequila in, as we thought it might be too harsh flavorwise—we weren't animals!—but we put the tequila worm in, having cut it into three, and gave Amy a jelly worm. Then, about nine, we set off into the freezing cold for the same pub as the night before. The first thing I noticed was that the monk wasn't there. In fact, hardly anyone who'd been there the night before was there tonight. Instead there were loads of people like us, people from out of town, who'd come for the views, for the cream teas, for the pencil sharpeners from the gift shops. Except we weren't like that, were we? We'd been there the night before, praying with a monk. We didn't have an SUV. We had Keith.

Just before midnight I tried to start a conga, but it was just the four of us who went for it, looking like the beginning of a game of Snake on an old Nokia. I'd love to see one person do a conga. I think even if they weren't shouting, "Hey guys! I'm doing a conga! Join me!" it'd be obvious they were a one-person conga. In a sense, though, any dancing is a one-person conga. So many congas must have started accidentally: what lone person is going to refuse a pair of friendly arms around their waist, ready for a jaunt around the room? Unless it's those horrible men who come up behind you when R. Kelly comes on, who are just snakes, full stop. No chance of anything like that in this pub. Defeated, we joined the limp "Auld Lang Syne," then plodded back to the cottage.

Things got a lot better once we'd settled back into our armchairs, which were still warm—in fact, it was as if we'd never left. There was some punch left. Our little group was united by the experience of having being in the pub with all those people who weren't like us. I looked at the others. It didn't matter that Amy was pregnant and Gav had taken up running.

"Ahoy regards, you crazy fuckers!" I shouted to them all. "I genuinely don't want anything more than this! This is one of the best moments of my life."

"Ours, too! Ahoy regards!" they echoed before immediately starting to peel off to bed one by one. I stayed in my chair, drinking port, gazing at the gas fire and imagining it was a real fire to complete the picture. I wondered what Sam was doing. He'd said he was going to go to a party. I wondered if he'd met some girl, if he was getting off with some girl in the room where everyone puts their coats and bags, the wooden button of a duffle coat digging into his flank. Maybe he had already forgotten about me. Maybe he'd returned the memory box while I was away, and Roy was lying in a landfill.

After a few hours, Amy padded down to go to the toilet and then curled up on the other sofa.

"I did think Sam was The One, you know," I slurred, staring into the bars of the gas fire. "And all the magazine surveys said that he was."

"Of course he was The One," Amy said.

"Oh, cheers!" I said, waving the bottle of port. "What do I do now, then? Go on to the Twos?"

"Nup," she went on. "I've got some good news for you."

"You're not having twins, are you?" I said.

She laughed. "Because he was The One," she went on, "the next serious relationship you have will be The Actual One. It's definitely true. It happened with me, and loads of people I know. When you think you've met The One, it means you've met The One Before The Actual One. It's like the final practice run."

"Bollocks," I said. "I don't believe there's just one One. If you're Anne from Edinburgh and your One is a Mexican farmer, what are the chances of you meeting? What if your One is blind, and you're deaf? No, I think there are a few Ones around. You just have to meet them at the right time, and both be prepared to put effort into the relationship. Romantic, huh? I think there are a few Ones, a lot of Twos, and a fuck of a lot of Threes. Anyone who believes there's one One for them who they haven't found, who thinks that's romantic, doesn't want a relationship. Which is fine."

"It's not some kind of mystic thing," said Amy. "I agree with you—I'm not saying there's only one Actual One. What I mean is that you both have to be completely ready to have that relationship. So there could be loads of guys who are suitable to be The Actual One, but the two of you have to meet at a time that's right for you. You only have to look at people. How can one guy treat his girlfriend like shit, maybe even cheat on her, and then you see him a year later and he's married and really happy? That seems like inconsistent behavior, but it's about him meeting that second girl at the right time. She's right, and the timing's right."

"Maybe," I said, taking a glug of port. "Now let me stare at the bars of the fire. I've only got a few more days to milk the just-broken-up-with-someone thing before I'm expected to behave like a normal human being."

She moved onto the sofa next to me and I dozed off with my head on her lap.

The next morning we packed and clambered into Keith, and then it was time for the obligatory visit to the beach before we set off back to London. I didn't much feel like going back. Sam was going to come round with the bloody memory box. I'd already plotted to keep his *Peanuts* book rather than returning it to him, but that was scant comfort in the grand scheme of things.

"Just for an hour," Mark said as we slammed Keith's doors. "The traffic's going to be horrendous."

"Are we just leaving all our stuff in the car?" I said.

Everyone laughed and said, "This is the country!"

"No one's going to steal your Daft Punk CD," chuckled Amy. "To prove it, I'll leave it in temptation's way."

She got it out and put it on the hood of the car. I let her. St. Davids didn't seem a place where there would be a lot of robbers. Everyone wore shoes caked with mud and drank unpasteurized milk. Also, they looked weather-beaten and wise. It's like when I'm on a train alone late at night after a gig and a man gets into the carriage—you're just slightly aware of it— and then if I see he's wearing glasses and has a bike, I think, *Phew! It's OK. He's got a bike. He's a nearsighted cyclist—not a man dressed as a robber.*

We ambled down in the fog and started to collect materials for a fire. Why we were trying to build a fire on a freezing beach when we had warm old Keith a mile away was beyond me, like when people sleep in a tent in their own garden. (Maybe I'm the only person who did that. I was fifteen and practicing to go to festivals.) Eventually we succeeded in making the beach fire, and you know that I don't care much for the sea and all its frills, but it was a lovely moment. I looked at everyone. Amy had dark circles under her eyes and looked pretty pasty. Gav was doing calf stretches. Mark was flicking between Facebook and a real-estate website on his phone, unable to decide which gave him more glee.

It's all right, I thought. *Nothing can break the ties of friendship. People don't fundamentally change. If I happened to run into the sea naked right now, they'd do the same. If someone does something like that, it's impossible not to follow suit. At the very least, even if they don't run in after me, they'll nick all my clothes and hide them behind a rock, and the slate'll be wiped clean. Like I've jump-started a car, they'll all wake up from this little dream. Sure, the baby'll come, but Gav won't end up doing the run. He's hardly done any training so far. Mark's just looking at properties for a bit of a laugh at dicks who buy houses. I'm going to do it. In a way, this is a hit for the team. I'm restarting the collective computer. I'm going to take all my clothes off and run into the sea. Now!*

When I turned back and saw that they'd barely registered, it was a terribly cold realization, figuratively and literally. My mates had grown up, and I had not.

7

Isy eats a Mars bar for old times' sake

Stationary in Keith on the motorway with my damp hair licking at the nape of my neck, I still felt like a bit of a twat for having just run into the sea naked. It's the kind of "spontaneous" thing one half of a couple does in a sub-sub–Woody Allen film, in the moonlight, tipsy. But I'd done it in real life, in broad daylight, in a state of sobriety, and in Wales. I was slowly absorbing the truth. It was irrelevant how many seas I ran into: things had changed, whether I liked it or not. A few of my other friends had kids, but none of my really close ones. I looked upon the ones who had them as proper grown-ups, like they must have had some kind of spiritual experience that persuaded them to do it, all that mopping up and oohing and ahhing and sleepless nights. Like they had something I didn't, like something or someone had given them the desire and skill to do it. For that matter, I viewed anyone who'd gotten married or bought a house in the same light. People who had a driver's license and could recall what day the recycling went out weren't far off. The Grown-Up Angel had visited them and told them they were going to have a baby and a mortgage and a wedding, and they didn't even have to go anywhere near gold, frankincense, or myrrh, whatever the fuck myrrh is.

But now it was happening to my best mates. Oh, how I'd wasted the years, not appreciating their carefree nature! Memories flashed before me: a Saturday night at Amy and Gav's old flat, us sending Gav out onto the main stretch in East Dulwich with an accordion and not letting him back in until he'd earned a fiver; the time I created a food version of *The Wicker Man* out of waffles and Jelly Babies; the time Amy and I wrote and performed a song (complete with dance) about how much Gavin loved Tottenham because he's an Arsenal fan; our onetime restaurant-owner landlord offering us vindaloo when the heating broke down; and all the parties—a party where we each had to bring a shopping cart for a massive shopping-cart fight in the garden; a party where we ended up doing a twenty-person conga in the street and I fell and got gravel embedded in my arm, then poured brandy on it and carried on; a party where I made up a game called Crevice Sex, where a line of people had to lie, fully clothed, spooning, and I would call, "All crevices present?," people would answer, "Crevice Mary present!" "Crevice Alan present!" and so on, and then I'd shout, "Let the crevicing commence!" and everyone would hysterically bang their nether regions into the person in front of them's bum, really quickly, for about five seconds. That was it. I'm well aware that it sounds like butt sex, but it was not butt sex. It was never sexual. It wasn't like the R. Kelly men. It was just totally ridiculous.

If Amy *was* right about The Actual One coming after The One, my next long-term relationship would be The Actual One, and I would be in the same club as everyone else. But what if a boyfriend before Sam had been The One and Sam had been The Actual One, but we'd given up too easily? Relationships took compromise, and faith, and grit. I knew what it was to buy two steaks and an extra-large bag of spinach. I knew what it was to get home and burn the meat slightly because you got carried away chucking handfuls and handfuls of spinach into a saucepan, yet when you looked at the bag there was barely a dent in it. To eat and drink too much, and have slightly burpy, acidic sex at the end of the night after naughtily watching *two* episodes of *The Wire* on a school night. To have pet names like Wuni Wuni that are the center of your world while you're together and that would cause you to instantly die of shame if anyone from the outside world knew them; yet that evaporate into nothingness within days of breaking up, so much so that within weeks of that momentous day, you can't remember those names at all, or songs you made up together, or patterns of speaking you shared. It's like they were only ever accidental, not particular to you two, just floating around in the ether for any old couple to grab. "You got Poo-chops? Aw, hard luck. Don't worry. It doesn't look like it'll be much more than an eight-monther. Hang in there, buddy. I mean, Wee-bum."

Or perhaps nature makes you forget them because it's like childbirth—you'd never do it again if you could remember.

I've even been known to recycle pet names when relationships have been back-to-back, to avoid the terrible beginning bit where you've got to use each other's *real* names, digging blindly like moles for some quirk or incident to hang a pet name on. It's much easier and simpler to recycle the name, especially if you're not sure about the guy. Just add or change a few letters. "Hallo, Mr. Snufflington!" you blurt out one morning, as if it's just popped into your head. While Mr. Huffington turns in his freshly dug grave, Mr. Snufflington is very much alive, kicking, and none the wiser. Although unlike Mr. Huffington, he doesn't like us brushing our teeth together or my eating prawn puffs straight from the freezer, which Mr. Huffington accepted without protest. Good old Mr. Huffington. Pity he reused the same piece of dental floss for a few days and snored so loudly.

Keith drew up at the good old service station, the scene of the crime only a few days previous. My hair had dried now, into fat, shapeless chunks. To everyone's surprise, I opted to stay with Moomoo and sent them off, under strict command to get me a Mars bar. I needed to think.

I started to run through all my exes, taking them out of their boxes, shaking the dust off, holding them up to my ear to see if they had any life in them. I'd had two long-term relationships in my life, including the one with Sam that had just ended; three between the six- and nine-month mark; and then a shotgun smattering of nonstarters, flings, and stolen moments, which sounds like a brand of shit chocolates. I disregarded those last three categories immediately. One bloke I'd snogged only because his name was Xander and I was on an alphabet challenge in East Grinstead. Two of them came out of the closet immediately after getting off with me—which I took as a massive compliment (I am the definition of Woman and if you don't like this booty, you won't like any). Some of them were from school, and I could barely recall them—a blur of clumsy kisses that tasted of cider and Embassy Filter cigarettes, things that happened while one of you was babysitting, buying matching T-shirts, sweaty palms on roller coasters, broken hearts that felt like they would never heal, and a prismatic myriad of terrible fingering techniques.

The three six-to-nine-month ones weren't worth examination, either. One had been at youth theater, and was only really because he was Kenickie in *Grease*; the second was with a guy from a call center I once worked at who said "groovy" a lot; and the third was with Tom, a musician who was lovely but not right for me.

So that left the long-term one that wasn't Sam—an on-off relationship with a guy in college that was fueled by lager and late-night chats about which Mike Leigh film we'd ideally be in (little did we know we were about to graduate straight into playing pigs, rats, ducks, and crack addicts in Theater in Education tours[*])—it was just one of those inevitable dramaschool things that happens, like orange leg warmers and

---

[*]When I was at drama school, I'd spend my nights imagining my hilarious acceptance speeches for my soon-to-be-won Oscars and BAFTAs, whose collective weight would eventually require me to reinforce my mantelpiece with steel. Little did I know that I was soon to graduate into the world of Theater in Education tours, where I, along with other desperate, twitchy goons, would pile into a clapped-out van with scenery and guitars at six in the morning daily in order to drive to different schools to perform shows like *The Doggie Who Lost His Tail (Then Realized All Animals Were Equal)* and *Hey, I'm a Molecule! What's the Matter?*

people dribbling with concentration as they try to become "centered."

Going through them, I could often only recall the end of each partnership, along with lonely moments or arguments. I guess this is often the way. When we think back over the whole thing, any genuinely good memories of time together—the day monkeys ripped the antenna off your rental car in the animal enclosure at Longleat Safari Park; the night you dressed up as a nurse in bed, and then you both got genuinely sidetracked talking about the pitfalls of the NHS while a third-rate hand-job took place in the background—are poisoned with the memory of that dreadful last day together. That day always starts off as a normal day. The birds are singing, there's still a horrendous pile of dishes to do—but one of you's got this leaden secret: you're going to end the relationship.

Say it's you. You're on your way over and he makes a salad because he doesn't know that anything's wrong (although of course he does), and for some reason it's so much more elaborate than usual—a *whole bag* of spinach, raisins, bits of apple, cranberry, chicken *and* halloumi even though they taste the same, massive flakes of salt—in a big bowl to eat out of at the same time, wedged into the sofa. You swallow taste-less chunks of gorgeous food, resting against his warm flank, knowing that you're about to plunge headlong into misery. I can understand why people do a U-turn at the last moment, especially when halloumi's involved. But with me, if I'm the one doing it, it just comes out whether I like it or not, and then life is totally shit for a while.

And inevitably when, years later, you think of him, you

think of that last day first, and the salad; or you do think of the monkey enclosure, but at the same time you feel angry about how you felt that he sometimes put work before you or didn't make enough of an effort with your mates, or you blame yourself for not making enough time for him, or for wanting everything to be just so. As we trundled along in Keith, I tried to balance it out with memories of lighter moments. Our childlike, disbelieving breathlessness as the monkeys climbed onto our shiny car, looked at us with reluctant malice rather than glee, as if we'd made them do this, and began beating bits of antenna repeatedly on the roof, my ex unable to move forward or in reverse for fear of killing one of the little shits. The moment we realized that our fiery debate about the initial hopes of the NHS versus a backward-thinking government had completely taken over what was supposed to have been a sexy moment, and couldn't stop laughing.

Having rifled through my scant file of past serious relationships, I came to the conclusion that Sam *was* The One—there was definitely nothing with legs previous to him that I'd missed out on. In fact, if anything, I'd probably wasted time trying to make relationships work when they weren't right. There's a part of my personality that exhausts all possible avenues thoroughly and only then makes a clear decision—it can be quite good workwise and in terms of sorting out old boxes of stuff, but in the same way I made myself try liver four times before deciding it was fucking disgusting, perhaps I'd spent a bit too much time with the wrong guys. The upside is that I never go back once we've stepped away from each other. This situation, for example, has never happened to me:

Whereas this has:

My research meant that because The One hadn't some-how bypassed me, there was no way Sam could be The Actual One, thank fuck. It would have been a bit of an inconvenience to have to tell him we had to stay together after all.

8

Isy discovers that famous people can stand next to flapjacks

I gazed out the window as we drove past the building with the massive bottle of Lucozade on the side that meant we were nearly back in London. It was the New Year now. Amy's tummy would grow, Gav's would shrink if he carried on running, and Mark's would soon be full of property information because his brain was about to overflow with it. As I wondered how I was going to get through the rest of my life, I got a text asking if I wanted to come to a party in Dalston,* a party mainly for

---

*At the time of writing, and based on the party I was about to attend, Dalston was an übertrendy hipster area of East London bursting with people who wear one red shoe and one green shoe, and coffee shops where the beautiful staff have sad red mouths like in a child's drawing, and restaurants where slivers of cheese are served on axes. Like in the game Hungry Hungry Hippos, hitting any of these components with a giant plastic mallet causes a similar thing to pop up half a mile away. Then you have to cart your giant plastic mallet onto the bus in order to hit the next thing, and, unlike with Roy in South London, the driver charges you extra.

people who hadn't been to bed since New Year's Eve. I felt instant relief. I could stave off reality for another twenty-four hours. In fact, I wanted to just go to Dalston and never come back, living off berries and my wits. I can understand those people who suddenly start again, wiping their lives clean by moving on their own to Germany or by putting all their belongings on eBay, although I'd pity the fool who ended up with my teenage poetry book:

> *Nothing is real, for the wolf cries out*
> *And still the world is lying, the world is lying.*

In about 1993, at the age of fourteen or fifteen, I went to see a live show by Rob Newman and David Baddiel of the TV comedy program *The Mary Whitehouse Experience* in Norwich with my friend Hannah. To our absolute shame, her mum had to drive us because we were so young, and it's hard to hitch from Matlock to Norwich because it's all winding roads. This was when Newman and Baddiel had done Wembley and were doing massive tours as a duo. We loved them. We chose Norwich because it was one of the smaller venues and we thought we had a higher chance of meeting them. We were right. After the show, we hung around. We'd never met anyone off the telly. Susan Tully, Michelle from *EastEnders*, was also in the show, and we saw her first. We followed her into the toilets and asked her for her autograph while she was still in the stall. Then we went into the café and Newman and Baddiel were there, just standing near some flapjacks. We couldn't believe it.

I'd brought reams and reams of poetry I'd written, including the poem above, in the hope of plucking up the courage to give it to Rob Newman. I genuinely thought he'd know a publisher who'd recognize me as the next Jackie Kerouac—although Jackie Kerouac sounds less beat poet and more Surrey divorcée who's rebuilding her life by trying quinoa for the first time and training to be a Zumba instructor. I chickened out of giving them to him, and Hannah's mum said she would if I didn't—she'd driven all the way to bloody Norwich for this—so I went over and handed them to him. Rob took the sweaty, thrice-folded bulk of horrific poetry and very kindly said he'd keep it, and that meant the world to me, because I was a teenager from Matlock, where nothing seemed to occur, and he was a man off the TV, where anything seemed possible.

Around that time I met another hero of mine, Jim Bob from Carter the Unstoppable Sex Machine. I first went to see them when I was thirteen and Samantha from the year above had a spare ticket. I thought they were incredible and must have seen them live about ten times throughout my teens, even though I invariably got into the stinking mosh pit at the front and got kicked in the head repeatedly with cherry Doc Martens and fainted and had to be hauled over the barriers and then deposited at the back of the crowd, only for me to weave my way to the front again for the whole merry cycle to repeat. That was when you could smoke inside, and I used to take twenty Benson & Hedges, twenty Marlboro Reds, and twenty Embassy Filters, just in case. Like when someone has a backup Mars bar in their glove compartment or a spare raincoat folded into their backpack. Just in case of what? Of sixty people suddenly needing their favorite brand of cigarette, in a life-or-death situation? I'd have each pack shoved deep into one of my pockets—right, left, and right bum—and then they'd get squashed when I was in the mosh pit, my body glued to other people's with sweat and lager, but we'd still smoke them when we got outside even though they were broken or bent sideways, the piercing cold air on our soaking wet T-shirts.

I got to meet Carter because of a girl I encountered on the coach bus. We used to get the coach from Derby bus station—the tickets we bought from Way Ahead Records included a return coach trip—and for some reason at that time, there was great rivalry between Carter fans and Morrissey fans, and often fighting. There were always loads of coaches lined up in the bus bays going to gigs, and they'd have to separate the Carter and Morrissey coaches with a few neutral ones like Dodgy and the Levellers. There might sometimes be a boyfriend and girlfriend where one was going to see Carter and one Morrissey, and the situation was like *West Side Story*. This girl who got me backstage had been across to the Morrissey fans as a kind of self-appointed ambassador, given out a few toffees, and gotten some poppers in return, and I thought she was the kind of person it would be good to get on my side. She told me she could get me backstage if I met her by the stage door after the gig, and I didn't believe her, but she did it.

She was just the type who, even after they run out of toffees to bribe people with, have one of those faces that gets places. It's not to do with being attractive—I believe it's to do with a mixture of unflappable confidence and having an extremely ordinary-looking face. I can think of a few entertainers and politicians who don't seem to have loads of discernable talent, but when you break it down, they've got those two ingredients, which is actually a talent in itself. People just didn't question her. Security and roadies actually made way for us. I, on the other hand, was the complete opposite. Pale to the point of translucence, with wary eyes slathered in kohl pencil, hair worn as over my face as possible and shoulders so rounded in an effort to be invisible that I was well on my way to being a little goth hunchback. When we eventually got to the dressing room and stood by the door, I was so nervous that I felt invisible, like I could feasibly climb into the wall, then through it, then back onto the coach and the warmth and safety of the hoi polloi.

Eventually one of the band's small entourage invited us to sit down, and the girl and I perched on the edge of the same plastic seat. I could not say a single thing. I couldn't even clear my throat or shift my foot for fear I'd fuck it up in some way. I couldn't believe that Carter the Unstoppable Sex Machine were actual people, sitting on chairs, who, like other humans, bought stamps and lost remote controls down the backs of sofas and stubbed their toes. At one point Jim Bob said, "Do you talk?" and I managed, "No." That was it. Then I gave him a cassette tape of my songs, which were like my poetry but put to music, if you can imagine such a thing. It had my address on it, and he wrote me a letter saying he liked them, and I kept it for ages in a shoebox covered in stickers that said things like I SURVIVED THE ISLE OF WIGHT!

At that point in my life, when I gave Rob Newman the poems and Jim Bob the tape, I felt on the brink of anything-dom. I was living in a small town and wanted desperately to make a living from being a writer and performer. It was statistically unlikely, but I had a spirited wonder about the world and trusted that if I kept trying and working hard, everything would be OK. That continued when I left Matlock. Throughout my twenties, I felt like anything could happen—I could become a lesbian! A pilot! A DJ! A cheese grower, like the guy from Blur!—and yet now, all these years on, it seemed that my best possible option was to settle for a bloke with baggage so heavy he had to pay additional fees. There was no point in his trying to wedge it into one of those frames at the airport to try to get out of it. There were issues spiraling out in all directions—he couldn't even get the zip done up. Whereas before, I'd meet someone and think, *He's fit! And he likes vine tomatoes rather than cherry ones? Let's go to the amusement park!*, if I met the same one now I'd go, *He's cute—so why is he single? Maybe his parents split up when he was eight, so he finds it hard to open up. He could already have a kid. How can I find out? Look at his phone. Shit, there's a four-year-old. Could it be his nephew, though? Is that as stupid as wondering if the woman he's holding hands with is his sister? And why is he eating vine tomatoes? Will he make me go to Borough Market every week and spend thirty-five pounds on fennel crackers? Run away!*

"BE ALL right, Is," Amy said from the front of the car. "I bet Sam had a shit New Year's." We were nearing London and I

realized I hadn't spoken for ages and had probably been looking moody and pensive.

"Yeah," added Gav. "Plenty more fish. Although maybe
you don't have to run in naked looking for them next time!"
Everyone laughed, including me.

I doubted Amy's Actual One theory, but if she was right
and there he was, waiting in the wings, the silly twat, gobbling vine tomatoes and kicking the curtain while he waited
for his cue, he could piss off for the moment. Despite what
they so obviously intended for me, I didn't want to be smug
and settled. If they wanted to play at being grown up, I wanted
to play at being a toddler. Before I met The Actual One and
settled into some half life, gradually submerging into the
world of rock gardens and ovulation and carrying an um-
brella at all times, I wanted to have some fun. I didn't want to
meet anyone new, snog anyone new or old, shag anyone at all.
There was only one thing for it. I had to hang out with people
who were also single, whose only agenda was to have fun. If
they happened to be a few years younger than me, so what? I
was definitely not ready for another relationship, so I didn't
care if the men were more like boys, puny and skinny-jeaned.
I didn't even care if they used moisturizer. I was going to stop
annoying my mates with talk of partying in multistory parking lots and swapping clothes with gay guys dressed as aliens.
I was just going to do those things, for real. I was going to go
out to a party in Dalston.

9

Isy downs Sambuca on a rope swing

I instinctively put my hands up to my face as the chants grew louder all around me in the dingy room, which reeked of ancient BO from vintage clothes.

"You! You! You've got the key! You! You! You've got the key!"

I was in serious danger of being a victim of Death by Hipster. And all I'd wanted was a night away from sensible people. I suppose I'd asked for it.

THE NIGHT had started normally, in a busy pop-up bar, which, I learned, means a bar that pops up for a few months in, say, an industrial park, then promptly pops down again when the going gets tough.

"What the hell does £15½ mean?" I yelled to my mate Caroline, looking at the board of drinks.

"Oh, that's just how they write 'fifteen pounds fifty' in Dalston now," she answered. I looked at some jam jars on the bar filled with a gray liquid sprinkled with what looked like cilantro. In for a penny, in for a pound. Well, for many a pound, in this case. Still, the night was looking good. I was with a small group of my mates who lived in North London but were from either Matlock or Liverpool, we were all up for it, and we'd decided to stop "for a quick pint" on the way to the party.

As the jam jar grazed my lips, I glanced around. People generally looked like a cross between La Roux and David Bowie, regardless of their gender. There were crayons on each table, and people were freely drawing and writing on the walls. From my seat, I read "Uncle Beats" and "Catch 22 Then Drop 22 (pills)." Were these people my new brethren? If tonight was a success, maybe I could move from Camberwell up to Dalston, start a band. I stopped biting my nails and smiled at a girl at the table next to us, who was wearing a cape and a tutu. She smiled back. It was all going to be OK!

"I like your tutu," I shouted. She smiled again.

"I like . . . everything," she said back. This was vague. Everything as in all my clothes, or everything in the universe? I was wearing jeans and a black top, which to them probably looked insane.

"What do you like best out of all my clothes?" I pushed, fueled by the contents of the jam jar.

"Um." She paused, her glittery eyelids downturned. "For your generation, it's not bad."

Not only was the party in an artists' commune, but it

would also feature rooms that contained "artistic happenings," Caroline informed me after we got into a cab.

"Right!" I said. "Artistic happenings." Maybe Banksy would be there! After a stop to buy Peroni and Sambuca because it was bring-your-own-booze, we drew up outside a large townhouse with loud music pumping out and a small queue outside. When we got to the front, we had to pay a tenner to get in—at least it wasn't £10½. Inside, it was absolutely rammed. It was like a cross between a fifteen-year-old's house party where she invites eight friends and the whole grade turns up (including someone in not double but triple denim), and the plays we used to put on as kids and charge our parents 20p to watch. Things like *The Lion, the Witch, and the Hamster Drawer*, which was a blatant C. S. Lewis rip-off with the sorry tale of the dead hamsters somehow shoehorned in and Aslan crying about it. Those plays were utterly serious, and so was this party.

We headed upstairs. I was nervous. It didn't look like it was possible to live there. There were ovens and fridges and sofas—they were just surrounded by things like mannequins in rubber outfits. Each room had a theme, like Feminine Bomb or Angels' Delight. I was relieved to see that at least the apostrophe was in the right place. They obviously had a copy of *Eats, Shoots & Leaves*. Maybe, like mine, it would be a nice surprise in their memory box. I remembered with trepidation that Sam was bringing the memory box over the next day. I took a gulp of Peroni and entered the Feminine Bomb room.

Stretched across the far wall was a white sheet showing a Pathé-style film on a loop, which everyone was watching. A

singer sang a cappella into a mic at the side of the room. In
the film, an animated spider was sitting on a big mushroom,
eating yellow stuff from a jar with a spoon. A little girl crept
up behind him, hit him on the head with her stiletto, and the
spider fell onto the ground, and then, as the girl sat and finished the yellow stuff in the jar, each of the spider's legs wig-
gled away from its body and slid in opposite directions.

"I don't think spiders' legs can do that!" I said proudly to
the woman next to me.

"It's not *literal*," she said, slurping from a jam jar. Since
this party was bring-your-own-booze, she must also have
brought her own jam jar.

I moved on swiftly to a room titled Alice in Wunderbarland. On a table outside the door of the room was a vial
of what looked like absinthe with a sign saying DRINK ME
taped to it, a few sweaty hot dogs on a paper plate with a bite
taken out of one, and a silver key that I discovered was actually tinfoil wrapped round a real key, which was already
silver. It was like Dungeons & Dragons, except real. Anything could happen! I took a drink from the vial, finding it
to be lukewarm blue WKD, and pocketed the key. The same
woman from the Feminine Bomb room noticed me do this.
I walked swiftly into Alice in Wunderbarland. Inside were a
few very tall performers dressed up as characters from *Alice
in Wonderland*—Alice, the Queen of Hearts, and the Mad
Hatter—and there were tiny plastic children's chairs upon
which people were sitting and chatting.

All of a sudden there was a crying noise from the corner,
which quickly rose above the chat. It became apparent that
a "scene" had begun. Everyone stopped talking and craned

round to see. Alice was sitting cross-legged on the floor in the middle of the room, crying.

"I'm Alice. I can't get home," she wailed. "Someone's stolen my rolling tobacco and my Underground pass." Big laughs. "And someone's stolen my key."

The jam-jar woman glared at me from across the room as my heart leapt into my mouth. A person dressed as a white rabbit hopped over.

"Oh, White Rabbit! You're here!" grinned Alice. I had to hand it to her—she was a good actress, going from tears to relief in a split second. Probably her height hindered her chances of working, unfortunately.

"Have you seen my key? Can you find the person who's taken my key? If I don't find it, I can't get home."

"What about your tobacco and your Oyster card?" a guy near me shouted good-naturedly.

"Well remembered, kind sir," countered Alice. "I need those, too."

"Here you go, Alice," said a guy from across the room, reaching behind his greasy ear and chucking a smoke at Alice.

"I love you, Alice!" shouted a girl who was wearing cat ears. "It's got seven quid on it, but sod it!"

There were murmurs of approval as she threw her Oyster card at Alice, who pocketed it.

"And here's your key," I shouted, throwing the key at her. I had an awful momentary vision of it glancing off the massive rabbit's head and stunning it, possibly killing it, but it landed on the floor near Alice. She stood up slowly, and smilingly pointed her finger at me.

"You, you, you've got the key!" she intoned.

Everyone around us immediately joined in, pointing at me. "You, you, you've got the key." How did they know what to do?

It's like when I get dragged to folk evenings with my parents and some old bloke stands up and sings, a cappella, something like:

> *Maisie's dancing in the scullery*
> *The soldiers went to war*

And everyone in the room gravely joins in with:

> *The horse is in the stables*
> *Won't be coming here no more,*
> *No more, no more,*
> *Dobbin won't be here no more.*

And I think, *How the fuck do you know the words?* And I look around as the folk song finishes and everyone's sipping real ale and looking at their hands introspectively, and I put the Stone Roses on my iPod full blast and look even more introspective and think, and my dad says, "Wake me when it's over."

"You, you, you've got the key!" they continued, pointing their fingers at me and grinning manically. I stayed rooted to the spot, bemused. After a few more chants, it died away and everyone began chatting again. As I started to leave the room, I saw the girl who'd given Alice the Oyster card go over and get it back. I went over, too.

"Sorry I took the key," I said, handing it over. "It just seemed like the right thing to do."

"Oh, that's the kind of stuff we *want!*" she said. "It's different every time. About an hour ago, everyone carried me on their shoulders out of the room. And just now, everyone started chanting, 'Alice? Alice? Who the fuck is Alice?' before I had a chance to finish the scene. It was hilarious."

A FEW hours later, sitting on a tire rope swing with Caroline, Bobby pouring Sambuca down our throats after twisting us around and around and then letting go, I surveyed the room. It's not like I was in any way on the lookout for The Actual One, as you know—I was actually seeing if The Actual One could be in the room so that I could escape him.

"Again! Again!" we screeched to Bobby, twirling round and round. To my surprise, the other partygoers were looking at us with mild disdain. I concluded that they wanted to be *seen* to be having fun, but our adolescent shrieks of glee were too obvious. I felt like they weren't really touching the sides—nothing was *literal*, so nothing really meant anything. Then I remembered how young they were, and that I had been the same at their age. The girl in the cape had been right about the difference in generation. They were all so thin, too! In my early twenties I was already curvy and cherub-cheeked, stretch marked with indigo, mauve, and violet. The stretch marks have now faded to white and become slightly raised, like braille. I always like to think that if I had sex with a blind man, he could run his hands over my inner thighs and bum and it would spell out the beginning of *War and Peace*.

The only guy who looked remotely like a potential companion for me was a tall, dark-haired guy, perhaps a few years older than the average here, his trousers held up by patchwork strips of material. I liked him because he was laughing his head off. Apart from him, I couldn't see anyone I wanted to talk to. They looked closed off, with their bright eyes and luminous leg warmers. Maybe I was a despicable person for judging all these hipsters in the same way a lot of them were judging us. See—there I was, judging them again. Maybe they *were* having fun and being themselves, in the most natural way they could. Just because it wasn't *my* definition of fun didn't mean it wasn't valid. And they were all different from one another. They were individuals, too. Then a guy smoking a pipe wheeled in a penny-farthing bicycle and I thought, *No, you're all twats*. What had I been thinking? That this party in Dalston would be the answer to all my prayers? That I'd magically transform into someone eight years younger, someone who didn't have any mates who were pregnant or knew about wild boar sausages? I didn't want to hang out at parties where everyone was eight years younger than me. I'd seen the people who do that. Standing out the more they try to fit in. Smoking cigarettes like people used to, holding them between their thumb and index finger. And on the dance floor, arm flaps in danger of taking flight as they throw "shapes" to songs they don't know. And at the end of the night, dreading the wrinkle-revealing bright lights of the kebab shop as they bump into fellow goons who never grew up, either, looking at them over the graying ribbons of meat and the chili sauce crusted onto the counter and thinking, *Shit, am I like you?*

I sighed, looking down at my shoes as we continued to spin on the rope swing. I didn't really want to make any new friends, did I? Deep down, I doubted the qualities of anyone who wanted to "make new friends" now. Anyone who hasn't got enough friends in their late twenties or early thirties would probably have something wrong with them. If someone describes one of their hobbies as "making new friends," it's scraping the hobbies barrel. If you're low on hobbies and a bit stuck, surely it would be more interesting to put something like "flying a kite," or even "going to the station" or "breathing." Unless you were raised by wolves or you're a French exchange student or you've spent the last three years locked in a room playing World of Warcraft and living off Ruffles and string cheese, "make new friends" should not be something that springs to mind when you think about what you like doing.

And there's already the problem of the existing friends on the periphery of your circle who you want to shake off. Any text conversation that contains the sentence "we must go for that coffee" and then remains in your inbox for two months because you can't bring yourself to delete it means there's something fishy about your relationship with that person. You promise to send your free dates, but when you look through your diary, you're unable to think how you'll both be able to sustain a conversation that lasts the duration of a weak latte.

The problem is that with technology now, it's really hard to dodge people who want to contact you. In the old days, people could call for you, or phone your landline. No one was going to write you a letter asking you to go see *Ghost* at the cinema that Friday unless they were loopy. But now there's mobiles, texting, and e-mailing, not to mention the shifting sands of social networking sites. You can't run and you can't hide, so you end up not only agreeing to meet someone from school you haven't seen for ages but also looking through photos of them at their wedding and on skiing and camping holidays, hypnotized by how much weight they've lost or gained and how much work you're getting out of doing in the meantime. I've left Facebook now, which was one of the best things I've ever done—I'd gotten to a point where I would idly flick through all the photos I was tagged in, knowing the order by heart, and how I felt about how I looked in each one. Now I use that time to find lip balm or dither about whether to have a bath, or I look up courses in ceramics and then decide against it. I still think that's healthier. I used to feel like shit after going on Facebook, like when you eat copious amounts of microwave food and think you're full but carry on and then half an hour later, miraculously you *are* hungry again and so you eat more.

I did an experiment before I left Facebook, because it took me a really long time to make the decision to do so. It was a few years ago that I left, and I still only get invited to about a third of the parties because there are so few of us not on it, but thankfully the ones I miss tend to be the ones where it's compulsory to bring homemade food. The experiment was that I set aside fifteen minutes a day for Facebook time. I'd make a cup of tea and sit down and go on it and not think about anything else while I was doing it. One of our teachers at drama school, Ian

Ricketts, once told me to do this with cigarettes when I used to smoke: to not do it repeatedly yet absentmindedly, half hating myself, but to set aside one slot per day to really enjoy one, sitting in my favorite chair or outside, and thinking about the smoke going down into my lungs and how it felt and what was happening inside my body. It really helped me give up smoking. Because the problem with social networking is that it's so easy to do, especially now that most of us have got it on our phones. It becomes like a reflex. I'll go for a wee without thinking, *Hey, I'm going for a wee. I'm reaching for the loo roll. I'm flushing the loo.* While I'm weeing I'm thinking about the mineral deposits around the bath or how proud of myself I am that I wash my hands these days even when it's just a wee. In the same way, I'd go on Facebook without thinking about it, half absorb whatever messages there were—someone I didn't know well inviting me to a book launch, or someone asking me to do a stand-up gig where the payment was sweets and cake (I get lots of these)— look at a few new photos of me and think that I needed to cut my hair, and then return to whatever it was I'd been doing, feeling a bit like I'd wanted something, I knew not what, but I certainly hadn't gotten it.

So. I did my fifteen-minute sessions. And what I found was that I couldn't really concentrate, because it's not something that's *meant* to be concentrated on. It's a half thing, like doing the dishes or watching *Wheel of Fortune.* Suddenly, when I was supposed to be enjoying and absorbing it, slowly scrolling through strangers' photographs seemed bizarre, almost sinister. The act of taking pleasure from the fact that someone I used to do finger painting with had gained a few pounds since then (of course he had—he was four when I knew him) seemed cruel. Searching for an ex to try to see if he'd taken his new girlfriend on holiday to the same places we'd been together seemed ridiculous. If he had, who cared? Babbacombe Model Village *does* deserve repeat visits. And now that I've washed my hands of it, I feel like I've gotten out of jail free. I can't believe I used to spend time deliberating over my profile photo, or what to put as my favorite music or TV shows. These change on a daily basis, especially as I have a terrible memory. I know I will always love the American *Office*, but I've also recently gotten into old Louis Theroux documentaries. So do I change the information on a weekly basis? For whom?

Most people I know are constantly trying to ditch an everchanging pool of two friends. My pool isn't ever-changing because I ever succeed in actually ditching them; it's because I constantly chicken out of actually doing it, and different ones get relegated at different times. The irony is, I'm probably in the very same people's To Ditch piles, but we're both dancing round each other constantly, asking, "How's your sister's master's coming on?" and "Remember five years ago when we went for fish and chips on the spur of the moment?" when we both really want to say, "You're great, but it's never quite clicked between us, and I think we're probably going to irritate each other a bit more every time we meet. I think we're fine in a group, when we're diluted, but I get a slight sinking feeling when we're in a conversation on our own and I do this thing to get through it where I kind of slot my thumb into a groove I make with my index finger. Don't worry, it's hard to describe, so I'll draw it."

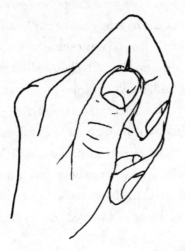

"You can keep the drawing. But yeah, I think we're both harking back to the past a bit. You feel the same? Oh God, if only I'd known that for all these years! I wish we'd told each other earlier! You know what? We're so similar! We must go for that coffee!"

ABOUT HALF an hour later, we had spun on the rope swing all we could, and Caroline and Bobby showed no interest in visiting the Alice in Wunderbarland room. We were getting ready to leave the party when the dark-haired guy from before skated over. Yes, skated. I'd been so distracted by the homemade suspenders that I hadn't looked down. I wondered if he'd skated all the way there, or if he'd changed into the skates at the door. I didn't know which was better. Maybe he'd been to a roller disco earlier. He looked like he might work at TGI Fridays, but he did have a nice face.

"My name's Joe, I live on a barge, you guys look like you like it large!" he said, shaking each of our hands.

"Yeah!" we said. "Do you want some Sambuca?"

"Well, my friend, don't mind if I do—which one of you does it belong to?" he said, swigging from the bottle. It dawned on me that he was speaking in rhyme. He coughed—not in rhyme, I noted—and handed the booze back to Caroline.

"Um, all of us, really," I said. I couldn't help thinking that he'd asked who the Sambuca belonged to only because he couldn't think of anything to rhyme with *do*.

"What's it like living on a barge?" Bobby said. "I've always fancied that."

"Well, my friend, in the winter it's cold, but it's a very fine life if you can withstand the mold."

I was silently impressed that he'd shoehorned in *withstand*.

He went on. "I wake in the morning and look out at the view; it's a very nice life if it's suitable for you."

Even he looked a bit downtrodden—from the heady heights of *withstand* to *view* and *you*. Still, I admired his chutzpah. And he actually only looked a couple of years younger than me. He had a mole very near his left eye that was a pleasing rich muddy color. He and I chatted for a little bit longer, him never wavering from the rhyming thing. I eventually gave in.

"Why are you speaking in rhyme?"

He grinned. "You ask me why I'm speaking in rhyme: I'd tell you the truth, but I don't have the time."

"You do, though!" I laughed. "What else have you got to do? Look around you!"

"We've got to go," Caroline said, shoving the Sambuca into my mouth for the last dregs. I got my phone out to call a cab.

"Hand on heart, it's been lovely to mingle," said Joe. "Before I go, are you . . ." Oh, God. He wasn't going to rhyme it with what I thought he was, was he? No, not *bilingual*. Although of course, I am—if you count "Tengo trece anos."

"I don't know," I said. "I am, but we only broke up on Boxing Day. I came to Dalston to forget everything, but it kind of made me remember everything."

I paused, then continued, "December wasn't a great month for me; at least I didn't go on a killing spree!"

He frowned and I stopped talking. Then he gently took my phone out of my hand and put his phone number in it.

"How have you got a phone?" I asked. "You live on a barge."

"You've got a lot to learn, miss," he said. And no, I did not give him a kiss. I'd had quite enough of everything for one night.

10

Isy is forced to pause Richard O'Brien's harmonica solo to listen to bullshit

I should probably take this opportunity to introduce my third housemate, Sue, who hadn't been on holiday with us at New Year's because it's her mum's birthday. She is very different from Amy and Gavin, and was integral to my life at this point because otherwise I'd just be living with a couple. Sue is a sort of lolloping, galloping girl, Roald Dahl–esque, with a loud, hooting laugh. One of the things I love most about her is that she never apologizes for her accent or her private education. She never judges anyone, and she doesn't change. Whereas I get into a cab with a Cockney driver and try to sprinkle a bit of London onto my Derbyshire accent, to pretend I'm his brethren. He doesn't want to be my brethren. Being my brethren isn't even on his mind. He considers the word *brethren* defunct.

Sue never wears makeup and has perennially rosy cheeks

and a slight breathlessness, like she's just taking a break from mucking out cows. She wears oversize men's shirts and rugby tops and refuses to don heels, even to weddings or funerals. She's the kind of person who has washed-in stains on their clothes that somehow manage to look classy and like they're meant to be there—otherworldly stains that I never recognize, like pheasant, and good red wine, and rich, manure-infused turnips that have been collected in a basket, then guzzled down with froth sucked straight from a cow's udder. These stains chuckle at Tide's and Clorox's efforts to overthrow them in the same way Zara laughs at H&M. She's the kind of person who would buy a raw rump steak from Sainsbury's and just eat it out of the packet there and then on the street, before wiping her hands on her jeans and asking what's for dessert. She has drinking competitions and arm wrestles with blokes, and she gets shit *done*. She has about ten brothers, all named things like Jake and Toby. Like me, she was single, and like me, she loved *Freaks and Geeks*, but this time, our viewing was being constantly interrupted.

"I don't get it, though," said Amy, rubbing cream onto her belly. "Why don't you just call Joe?"

"Yeah!" Gav chirped. "He wouldn't keep up the rhyming thing for a whole date."

I pressed pause on James Franco's lopsided smile.

"Look," I said, "I know you want me to go on a date with a guy from Dalston who speaks in rhyme"—I wondered, as I often do when I'm speaking, if that exact sentence had ever been uttered before, and concluded that it hadn't—"but (a) I only met him last night, so I need time to think about it, and

(b) I can't help thinking this is about you living vicariously through me."

"No!" they squealed in unison. "We just think you should have some fun after Sam."

Amy rubbed the cream in more vigorously. It was homeopathic, she'd said.

"You shouldn't rub that onto your whole stomach," I said, "just point-one percent of it."

She ignored me. "I'm doing pelvic-floor exercises as we speak! You can't tell, can you?"

I scrutinized her face through my banging headache. Every few seconds, a slight twitch took place near her right eye.

"You're twitching," I said. "Near your right eye."

She and Gavin burst out laughing. "Lucinda said that'd happen!" she said.

"Who's Lucinda?" I said.

"Oh," Gav chimed in. "Lucinda's the lady who's going to be running our childbirth classes." Sue and I exchanged glances.

Gav always uses the word *lady* when he feels in awe of someone, or when they're a lot older than him. I pictured a seventy-year-old hag with a house made of sweets in Peckham, beckoning young couples into her lair with her one shriveled finger; the blokes in Kings of Leon T-shirts and apologetic beards and the women twitching almost imperceptibly below the right eye, offering her Cath Kidston hand lotion in exchange for chamomile tea and breastfeeding cushions.

"We're not starting the class for ages, but we bumped into

her at the farmers' market and recognized her from Facebook and she gave us a few tips," said Amy.

"Oh, right," I said airily.

"Lucinda's got four kids under ten and she looks great," Gavin said. He looked at Amy, then looked into the middle distance, shaking his head like a mystic.

Please don't say, "I don't know how she does it," I thought.

"I don't know how she does it," he said.

"Well, crack addicts do it!" I snapped. Why do I always cite crack addicts in situations like these? In my world, crack addicts can get pregnant the first time; they can multitask and prioritize, e.g., getting crack is more important than eating, or doing a sudoku; and they don't rub homeopathic cream that probably smells like rotting undergrowth (not a euphemism) into the area above their healthily functioning undergrowth (euphemism).

"Why do you think she needs to call Joe?" said Sue. "Loads more exciting things than that have happened in the last twenty-four hours, like the Alice in Wonderland Oyster card thing!"

"And getting back the London Zoo ruler I'd forgotten about," I added.

Sam had been round that morning to give me the memory box, and, as with all these types of things, it had been slightly less awkward than I'd imagined. He'd handed over the memory box, I'd handed over his stuff in a Sainsbury's bag, and we'd had an awkward cup of tea in the kitchen, with Amy, Gav, and Sue coming in and out and feigning casualness as they did so. The contents of the memory box were scattered over the living-room floor. No penguin. Sam had said he would return Roy another time, when he could borrow his mate's car. I hadn't pointed out that I'd taken Roy to his on the bus. It all seemed so long ago now.

"She should call Joe because," came the reply from the direction of Amy and Gavin's sofa, "he could be The Actual One."

I don't know which one said it, and it didn't really matter. Recently they'd started to do that thing couples sometimes do, completely subconsciously, that demeans both components of the couple and also you, where one member of the couple laughs in a sort of secret way and says, as if they're divulging gold, something like, "*We* don't like olives." Or "*We* really think Bruce Willis has aged well." Really? You both think that, to exactly the same level? There's nothing more effective at banging home the fact that they're double, as it were—interchangeable, two peas in a pod—and you are single.

I don't like the term *single*, because it implies that you're one half of a yet-to-exist unit, like those necklaces your boyfriend nicks for you when you're fifteen, where one of you has one half of a heart and the other, the other, and once you've lost your virginity to him, you wear it on the outside of your Naf Naf sweater. When I started comprehensive school at eleven, the love token du jour was either one of those necklaces or *Forever . . .* by Judy Blume, which was an almighty book because it contained sex, like *Dirty Dancing* contained sex, and all our minds contained sex.

Sex when you're single can be the best or worst thing in the world. It can be everything or nothing. In a long-term relationship, sex is around, like a slightly dodgy electric fire you sometimes decide to put on on a Thursday night when you're watching *Man v. Food*, and you both go, "Oh, it's quite nice, actually—we should do it more often!" Sex when you're single is, in principle, exhilarating. That feeling when you're in a bad relationship and you look at someone who isn't in a relationship and you think, "My God, they're so lucky! They can have sex with anyone, literally *anyone* in the whole wide world! Why aren't they doing it now? I wouldn't be mooching around discussing Keane and eating a bacon sandwich, I'd be banging someone from Colombia or Leeds up against a car!" The grass is always greener, and sometimes there's no grass at all, which is frankly mental on a guy and heartbreakingly unnecessary on a woman. Mow if you must, but don't mow it all off. I'm saying don't pay twenty-five pounds for a procedure so painful it requires two aspirins on the way there and a double whiskey on the way back.

When you're single, some people assume that all you want to do is put on a meringue dress, sit on a white pony, and get married, like Jordan does every Saturday. Any drunken snog you have, with any dickhead, is elevated to high status—even if they've seen you snog the dickhead, and can see that he's a dickhead; even if he's got an actual dick grafted onto his head, in the wrong place, on his chin, or in front of his ear, all you get afterward is, "So, what's happening with Dickhead? Are you seeing Dickhead again? He lives in Fulham, doesn't he? It'd only take you fifty-five minutes to reach Dickhead—that's good for London!" Of the unhappy people I know, more are in relationships than single. It's not so black-and-white as to say that no one who's single is looking for a relationship, but you can be content and have your eyes open. You can be happy in your own company, as I was.

Yet when you *are* single, the issue of sex can be really frustrating. It can be frustrating because you're not getting any, and you don't know what's wrong with you, and suddenly even the rickety old electric fire from all those years ago seems so warm and inviting. And if you are getting some, but you're not in a relationship, it can be delicately brilliant, or mind-bogglingly complicated. I think the complications come about because of what sex can mean. The most common problem in my experience is that one person likes the other one more, but there's no relationship as such, and also no one's being quite honest. This is definitely easier to deal with in the summer months, when you can put on a new blue dress and gaze at your freckled arms and think, *Yeah, I'm all right!* And you go to the pub and drink cold beer and have a burger, and everyone's in a good mood, and you think, *So what if he puts one less kiss than me in his texts*, or he thinks, *Who cares if she avoids conversations about whether we're "seeing" each other or "going out,"* and you trip home merrily together and all is in harmony—even the hedgehogs and frogs are thinking the same: *So what if she throws herself into the path of a car when I mention building a nest together?* and *Who cares if he says he'll never move lily pads again after the incident in 1995?*

There's something nice about living in the moment, but that can only happen if there's no shit going on in your head. I hadn't had sex for a while—so it was high time to have some low-quality sex with someone I'd never see in daylight, or ever again. It couldn't be Joe, because there was something about him, and I wasn't ready for a relationship, or even a fling. I didn't want to play into the hands of Amy and Gavin. Wouldn't they just love it if I settled down with Joe? It had to be tacky, messy, and anonymous—as far away from couple-dom as possible. And I was in luck, folks. A few days later, I was going to Plymouth. And as Sartre said, if you can't get laid in Plymouth, you must be a ghost.

11

Isy plays pool with soldiers and makes friends with an old man

Christmas stand-up gigs are mostly difficult to perform at, as the audience is hammered, and January gigs are mostly weird, as the audience is broke, so they're often sober, or just not there. Nevertheless, only a hair's breadth into the New Year, here I was on a long car journey again, this time to do a gig in Plymouth. I was in the car with the other two comics: a puppylike Australian called Mickey and a posh English guy called Ross, who was driving. Car journeys can be quite full-on and tiring if you're with a load of comics you've never met or one you don't get on with, but they can also feel like a proper road trip if the combination is right, and this was. Despite the fact that we didn't know each other very well at all when we climbed into Ross's car—in fact, I think Mickey and Ross had never met—it became clear that this gig was going to be really fun.

People are generally fascinated by stand-up. There's often a belief that comics must have experienced some bad childhood incident to make them want to do it, but, traumatic as the hamster business was, I don't think we're these screwed-up hermits, as some newspaper articles would have you believe. However, a comic has to have an absolute need to go back onstage the night after a bad gig. You either want to do that or you don't—there's no middle ground. You either try stand-up and don't like it enough to give up your friends, relationship, and entire social life, or you try it once and subsequently give up all of the above to pursue it. That's why there will be some comics you don't think are great—they just had the discipline to do it—and some who are geniuses but who give up because they can't handle the ups and downs, or the monotony of doing the same material every night. You either fall in love with it at first sight or you don't. If you do, you say no to being a bridesmaid so you can sit in a car with strangers for a fourteen-hour round-trip to Torquay to do ten minutes for no money. You reject a holiday in order to go die on your arse at an agricultural college in front of student farmers who don't see the irony in your song about very right-wing villagers who assume that any male outsider who doesn't drive a Volvo is a pedophile, and kill him. (It's not as bleak as it sounds. I yodel the word *pedophile* repeatedly in the chorus.)

For years after you start off, you're doing most or all of your gigs for no money and have a day job, too. I was still surprised to actually be making a living from doing stand-up and acting. Until a few years earlier, I, along with a load of other "struggling artistes," was working for an ailing meal-delivery company in Battersea. The company was running out of money and had moved to a kind of corrugated iron shack with no windows on an industrial estate. We all worked on the phones, taking orders and checking where deliveries were. Most of our time was spent chasing deliveries. Wealthy people in the country would have ordered a three-course meal for ten—the address would be something like: The Old Rectory, The Green, Haverstock-o'er-the-Mound, with instructions like, "The driver must telephone as he reaches Tipperton Cross—our housekeeper Penny is hard of hearing and it will give her ample time to attach her wooden leg and make her way down from the wing"—and we'd get a flustered phone call at ten to six saying that the gravlax and beef Wellington hadn't arrived. We'd ring our delivery company to ask where it was and the driver would say that it hadn't left the depot in the first place, or that he'd left it "by the man." The outcome was never good.

A van came to the industrial park every day to sell lukewarm, soggy pies while our nice, suited boss did his level best to stop the business from going under. Born as Phil, he had legally changed the spelling of his name to Fyl during a hippie phase earlier in his life, but it was still pronounced "Phil." Fyl stood for Free Your Life. Every day, corporate-type people would ring up and ask us if we could put them through to "Fly," which would be a pretty good name for an American hip-hop artist, but Fyl was from Welwyn Garden City and drove a Citroën Zara. My route to work involved a short walk down a dingy, shrubbery-lined alleyway to get onto the industrial park, where mini-islands of detritus teeming with vermin dwelt like evil stepping-stones and where once, at 8:45 in the morning, I swear I heard from behind the bushes a male voice say, "Can I go . . . down below?" and a giggling female reply, "That rhymed, Barry!" Basically, we were creative types living the kind of life that I assume Dostoyevsky niftily sidestepped. Slurping black coffee and poetically gazing into the middle distance of the industrial park, I'd be interrupted with a tap on the shoulder and a question about the gift-voucher Excel sheet.

And late every afternoon, I'd clamber into yet another pastry-spattered Honda and shake the hand of a fellow newbie, and the Excel sheet and the angry food customers would fade away as we drove closer to the venue and my stomach started to somersault. We'd ask ourselves how the elements of the gig would work. What the layout of the room would be like. It's lethal if they're on round tables, as half of them are facing away from you. It's lethal if there's no lighting onstage. It's not good if there's no mic stand when you play the guitar, because you can't hold a mic, too, unless you've got a phantom limb that also works. (At Stoke University Student Union, they suggested plastic-wrapping the mic to my chest so it stayed in place, but luckily some kindly chump volunteered to crouch down and hold the mic for the whole set.) Yet with these gigs, you never ask yourself why you're doing it, why you're continuing to see the positives. You just do it. And then, having previously wondered how you'd ever do more than seven minutes, you do the Edinburgh Festival.

The Edinburgh Festival is a slog. For anyone who's not been there, go and watch stuff. It's brilliant. For anyone who

wants to perform there, it's a monthlong jamboree of pleasure, heartbreak, and madness. There are thousands of
shows in venues like church halls, hotels, and even swimming pools, ranging from one-person plays about Bad Stuff
That Can Happen to fifty-person dance pieces about engi-
neering. There are billions of people handing out flyers in
the streets from early in the morning, and the bars are open
all night, so as you stumble home over the cobbled streets as
dawn breaks, some eighteen-year-old dressed as an emu will
leap into your field of vision, screeching, "Awight, guv'nor!
Fancy seein' a Cockerney version of *As Yer Like It?*"

I didn't realize until I started performing comedy at
Edinburgh that unless you're a very big name you have to
be prepared to lose thousands of pounds each year, possibly tens of thousands if you don't sell well. This is because
of the often-astronomical hire for the venue, the charge you
pay on each ticket, getting photos and posters done, entry
into the guide to all the shows, a PR company to get people in
and hopefully shield your paper-thin ego from bad reviews,
and, unless you're insane, beer money. And chip money.
Some acts enroll at a gym on the first day and don't drink for
the month and go to bed at eleven o'clock every night, and
I look upon them with a weird mixture of admiration and
pity. The best and worst things happen late at night during
Edinburgh. I've stolen a croissant from a twenty-four-hour
café table at about three a.m., only to find its owner pulling
a (blunt-looking) knife on me on his return from the toilet.
(I managed to placate him by talking about the early work of
the Doors.) I've successfully auctioned to a group of drama

students a giant doll with moving eyes instead of nipples that a fellow comedian gave me as a birthday present.

Every comedian's got a Worst Gig Ever, and mine occurred at Edinburgh in a show called the Comedy Zone, when I hadn't been doing stand-up for long. The Comedy Zone is on every night of the festival in a large room and consists of four new acts doing twenty minutes each. It has a long history, and some really great comics have played it. At the beginning of the festival, I realized for a start that I barely had twenty minutes. I had about sixteen minutes, including a pretty bad bit about putting tabloid models addicted to heroin into the *Big Brother* house, and a long, meandering story about feeding a squirrel in a park in South London and an old man talking to me about said squirrel biting my palm. So at the top of my set list, to make it up to twenty minutes, I started writing the word *banter*. *Banter* should never be written in a set list. It is like writing *greet cashier* or *steal one grape* on a shopping list. It either happens naturally or it doesn't. You can't plan it, and you certainly shouldn't be listing it as material. But I had no choice.

The three other acts and I dwelt in a cramped dressing room adorned with posters of previous performers at the venue, some of them very famous, invariably with *twat* or *dick* written in pen across their foreheads. Carved into the wall where you stood as you were about to go onstage were phrases of encouragement like, "You won't always be shit!" and "Don't trip over before you reach the mic!" and "Bill Hicks started somewhere!" I used to walk on to the Eels, and I could always tell that I was going to have a good gig if people were bopping or singing along as I walked on. This didn't happen much, but it did happen once with a bachelor party all dressed as Banana-man, which gave me a fleeting hope in humanity.

The night of my Worst Gig Ever occurred about halfway through the month. It was a Saturday night, it was packed, and the room had a really ripe feeling, like the swelling just before a storm. Some gigs pootle along like an old car, with no big laughs but no real dips—just, I suppose, reasonably pleasant for all involved. Tonight wasn't like that. Tonight was going to go one way or the other, but it was going to go a definite way. The MC, Mark, introduced me—I was up first. I could see as I walked the short distance to the mic that the audience didn't know the words to my Eels song. Over the weeks up there, my "banter" had evolved into a series of "Give us a cheer if . . ." statements, which filled a few minutes and also gave the impression of energy in the room, even if it was only a feeble cry that lasted a few seconds. It wasn't laugh-ter, but at least it was collective noise.

Me: Hey guys! Give me a cheer on three if you're Scottish! One, two, three! Give me a cheer if you're English! One, two, three! Ooh, it's like *West Side Story* here! Though I'm not sure anyone's ever been knocked out by a haggis!

Silence and general confusion.

Me: Give me a cheer if you're Spanish! *Uno, dos, tres!*

Silence.

ME: Right! No Spanish! OK. Does everyone know what a
squirrel is?

SCOTTISH GUY NEAR BACK: You're shit. I hate you. This is shit.

Now. People think heckling's a lot more common than
it is. Sometimes, in less combative circumstances, people
heckle to "help" you or because they think it's a conversation. So, for example, you'll be onstage about to do your
cat material and you'll say, "I bought a cat last week," and
they'll blurt out, "Me, too!" as if you're on a date with them
and they can't believe this godsend, this coincidence. These
people must be treated gently and are not malicious. They
are at best stupid, and at worst actors. Yet the average person wouldn't heckle. You have to really want the attention to
heckle. It's a major exercise. When things go wrong and an
act is dying, most people sit cringing into their lager and
crisps, simultaneously bewitched and repelled by what's
happening onstage, the comedian becoming more and more
determined to win back the crowd or perhaps insulting
the crowd, saying they don't get the jokes. It's fascinating.
It's fascinating for comics, too, really, once we can put our
egos aside. How can material that normally works in a variety of rooms suddenly fail us? It makes you realize how
much of it is about trust. However, tonight I was not using
material that normally worked in a variety of rooms. I was
using material that would be clinging on by the skin of its
teeth even at a gig where people wore homemade clothes and
played Scrabble in the interval.

I tried to carry on with my set.

ME: If you don't know what a squirrel is, I can explain—

SCOTTISH GUY NEAR BACK: You're shit.

ME: I'm half Scottish!

SECOND SCOTTISH GUY: You're half shite!

SCOTTISH GUY NEAR BACK: You're totally shite!

The first laugh of my set.

ME: Right, I've only done three minutes, and I'm supposed
    to do twenty. If the show overruns, we get fined, and the
    most I can do is twenty-two. I could come off at eighteen
    minutes, but just to piss you off, I'm going to do twenty-
    three. Now—do you want a song about Jamie Oliver, or a
    song about a pedophile visiting Tunbridge Wells?

Silence.

SOUND GUY: Um. Pedo!

ME: Thank you, Simon. I've given away the punch line, but I'm
    doing it anyway. *(sings)* I live in a village, a very small vil-
    lage . . .

Before this onstage death, I thought I'd died before.
There were many times I'd been on in the basement of
a dingy Soho pub in front of a few other acts, a Bulgarian
family, and the mother of the guy who runs the gig, and
people try so hard to laugh, which is as hard as pretending to sneeze convincingly—you can do it for a bit, but then
your face goes, "Come on, mate"—and I'd thought then that
I'd died. I thought on those occasions when I'd tried a new
bit and people had just stared at me with searching, pitying
eyes that I'd died. But none of that is dying. It's just absence
of laughter. Dying is when the air actually seems to thin,

when you have an out-of-body experience and look down on yourself at the mic and you can only hear your own tinny voice, which sounds so unfamiliar. This was the first time I'd died in a big room.

Scottish guy near back: I hate you so much. I'll pay you to get off.

His wife: Erm—we paid a tenner to get in—

Scottish guy near back: No, Ruth, this is so bad, I've got to do something. For the sake of all of us.

People around him: Yeah!

Scottish guy near back: I'll pay you twenty quid to get off!

I pause, strum the trusty D chord again, and look at him.

I hadn't gone full time with stand-up at that point. I was working in the call center, and twenty pounds was a hell of a lot of money to me. In a way, this would be "earning money from stand-up," wouldn't it? I was standing on a stage, talking, and someone was going to give me money. In fact, they were giving me a pound a minute! The fact that he was giving me money to stop talking was a small detail.

Me: OK.

It took ages for my "fee" to snake its way through the crowd, during which time I genially fingerpicked in A minor on the guitar. Some people started to sway from side to side: now that it had been decided that I was shit and they had been saved, they were prepared to listen a bit. When I finally got the money, I didn't know how to get off. The fact that it was a tenner and two fivers made it somehow worse. Finally:

ME (*reverentially*): Fuck you, Edinburgh! Good night!

I strode offstage and into the tiny dressing room, where the ashen faces of Matt and Russell, the other acts, awaited me. "Tough crowd!" I mumbled, glimpsing the "Bill Hicks started somewhere!" carved into the wall. I wondered if Bill Hicks had ever been paid to get off. I immediately burst into tears, which has only happened once since—after a horrendous solo show in Whitehaven when a group of blokes wouldn't stop making snoring noises for the whole hour—and then I went and spent the whole twenty pounds on whiskey. I'm sure that's what Bill Hicks would have wanted.

THE GIG we were at in Plymouth, downstairs in a little bar near the center of the city, was lovely, although there was a Spanish guy in the front row who followed every punch line with, "Oh, really?" He meant well and, I think, genuinely wanted to know the answer every time. Immediately afterward, Mickey, Ross, and I dropped my guitar and a few bits off at the B and B, then headed to the Walkabout Plymouth, part of the UK-wide chain of Australia-themed pubs. Mickey was able to head there without thinking about it, like a homing pigeon. This was because he knew the fellow Aussies who worked behind the bar there. In fact, he said, he knew an Aussie in almost every Walkabout in Britain. The three of us walked in and Mickey was treated like a soothsayer: he told tales of what was happening back home as fellow Aussies gathered round and listened.

After our first couple of pints, the staff let Mickey behind the bar to pull some more pints for us. It was like *Cocktail*, apart from the fact that we were in a Walkabout in Plymouth on a Saturday night surrounded by rutting stags and crying hens, formed in gaggles of drunken frog spawn; one of them suddenly spilling out sideways to fall over or try to hit someone, only to be absorbed back into the group a few seconds later. One would escape for a dance or a cigarette and would be followed by a few of its mates, stumbling like newborn foals on the sticky floor. There were nurses, cavemen, and policewomen. There was one hen party all wearing pink feather boas—presumably to act like a badge on a school trip, so that if one got lost, she could be returned to the group safely. They weren't the best-made boas, so everywhere you looked on the floor there were trails of salmon-colored feathers, giving evidence as to where they had been, like in "Hansel and Gretel." The trail normally led the short distance to the toilets and was followed by more trails as it was duly pursued by fellow feathered hens clutching sparkling handbags and bright yellow drinks, their glazed eyes dull in their swollen, crimson faces.

I can't really handle many more than three pints of normal lager or two of premium, much to my chagrin, and we'd only had a few chicken nuggets at the gig for our tea. Now I'd had four or five pints and was in that state where you gaze at everyone around you and use them to make profound conclusions about the beauty or horror of humanity, usually in the safe knowledge that you're going to eat a greasy kebab soon. Whenever you see drunk people clinging to posts and looking slowly around, smiling and nodding to themselves, that's what they're doing. Pity you can never remember any of these philosophical thoughts even moments later. I watched a woman from the feather-boa hen night chatting to the bouncer, who she obviously knew well. She was utterly, utterly hammered. Unbeknownst to her, she had about twelve Sambuca-marinated pink feathers matted into her hair, and as she swayed around and talked to him, he gently picked each one out without her realizing and kept them squashed in his palm so she didn't notice. "God, that's so moving," I breathed to Mickey and Ross.

Even in my pissed-up state, I didn't feel that there were any males in the room ready for The Suttie Experience, so we headed to an all-night pool bar. It was a taxi ride away, and we wolfed down some chips and then got into a cab, still clutching our pints. The driver either didn't notice or didn't care. God, I wanted to move to Plymouth! By this point, it was probably about two a.m. The pool bar was quite small—there was a bar at the bottom of the stairs with a seating area, then a pool table down one side of the far wall. In the bar were: a group of three guys and three girls in their early twenties who were being quite loud; a short guy in a tracksuit that didn't match, who was alone but looking at everyone like he was just about to start speaking to them, then looking down and shaking his head; and an old man sitting on a barstool up against a wall with a plastic shopping bag at his feet, talking to himself. It was like a play, or a game. We decided that a couple of pints and then whiskeys would be the best option. I had a proper second wind due to the chips and suggested that we stick a vodka in the top of each lager, remembering with a smile that the last time I'd done that, I'd gotten someone to draw around me with Magic Marker on a wall.

"Gla ti si yeravana maaan drin," I heard. I turned round. The old man was grinning at me, his mouth a dark grave-yard with no headstones. He had deep wrinkles all over his face and ears almost the length of his head that were slapped on like an afterthought. I couldn't believe how long his ears were. Had they grown at the same rate as his head, or had his childhood been a complete nightmare?

"I'm sorry," I said, feeling pathetically middle class, "I didn't understand what you said."

He opened his mouth wide. "GLA TI SI YERAVANA MAAAN DRIN." A few people from the big group glanced over. My drunken mind raced. Was it code? Did they have their own language in Plymouth? I couldn't remember. I smiled and nodded.

"Yeah!" I said, clinking glasses with him, hoping I hadn't inadvertently promised to give him all my worldly goods or make a penguin for him. He picked the shopping bag up off the floor. His shoes, in contrast to the rest of his clothes, were immaculate. They had been polished hard. The bag was a Woolworths bag—I was quite impressed he still had one.

"SACKS!" he shouted, pushing the bag into my face. I looked inside. There were about ten pairs of men's socks, a Creme Egg, and a library book called *Ghosts of Biggin Hill*.

"Nice one!" I shouted back. We clinked drinks again. This was fine, wasn't it? It could just carry on like this. I mean, he wasn't a contender for the bedroom department, but I was losing hope anyway. Maybe this was better.

"GLA TI SI YERAVANA MAAAN DRIN," he said again, pointing to my pint in front of me on the bar.

"Oh!" I said, relieved. "'Glad to see you're having a man's drink'!"

I refrained from pointing out that I had just as much right to drink a pint as a man did, and that I'd always drunk pints. I just gazed into the black hole that was his mouth as he showed me some pictures from *Ghosts of Biggin Hill* and tried to detect the different notes in his breath. I got: raw meat, Guinness, and waffles.

Mickey, Ross, and I started playing pool. I was in that lovely, anything-can-happen zone of drunkenness now, and I was playing quite well. Because it was the three of us, there was a rather complicated system of me swapping from Mickey to Ross with each go, until one of the men from the group in their twenties offered to play, too. We got talking to them—they were soldiers from a nearby army base on leave. A few minutes later, their girlfriends came over and sat on each of their knees in sync. It was like *Memphis Belle*. I was fascinated, as I'd never met a soldier—there was a guy at college who'd claimed he went to Sandhurst for "a summer" and had gone on a night forest exercise where he was being chased and that resulted in his mistaking a cesspool for a sandpit and jumping into it, but then it turned out he'd only been in Boy Scouts—but I was shy of asking them stuff about their jobs. "Do you really have to carry stones in a backpack and run for a thousand miles?" "Do all the men have mustaches, like in the films?" That would be as annoying to them as when people ask what heckle put-downs we have, or what it's like being a woman in comedy. That said, whenever I meet a doctor socially, I do tend to ask them about a mole on my arm that has a dual hair growing out of it. They always look incredibly nonplussed and say that it looks completely fine. They and I know the truth: that I've only shown it to them so I can show off about the dual hair.

I've always had little bits and bobbles all over me—it's like my skin is prone to being a bit like the surface of the moon. I was born with a lump above my right eye that pressed the eyebrow down, making me look permanently grumpy. My mum was advised by the local vicar to hit it repeatedly with a Bible, but thankfully it sank into my face when I was a toddler. As a child I had various scatterings of spots and measles and poxes that graduated into eczema nestling under my earlobes and in my elbows and stress lumps popping out and in under my armpits. I got impetigo when I was about twenty-three. If you don't know what impetigo is, what happens is that you think you've got a spot, it looks ready to squeeze but nothing'll come out, the next day it's slightly bigger, the next day it's slightly bigger than that, and so on, until about four or five days later it's the shape and size of China and stretches from your mouth to your cheek. When I went to the doctor, he said that he'd only heard of me, children, and Amy Winehouse getting it.

The worst thing I've had in the bits and bobbles category started innocuously during one Edinburgh Festival. Again, what it initially looked like was a trusty old spot just above my left eyebrow. It grew and grew—however, not outward this

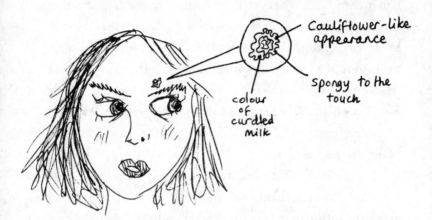

time, but forward. Over Edinburgh it valiantly bloomed, like I was watering it every day, and by the end of August, when the festival finished, it looked like a miniature cauliflower stuck onto my head.

I went to the doctor and she said it was a wart, and I had to go to King's College Hospital in Camberwell for treatment. The doctor there was very kind to me and said it didn't look like a cauliflower at all, just like a multicolored acorn, and he put some kind of acid on it. He said that in the next few days it would turn black, and then it would just fall off.

"Hopefully not into your Rice Krispies, otherwise you might end up eating it!" he added jovially as I left the room. I'd cut my bangs to cover the wart, but it was windy, so I had to hold them down with my index finger as I walked along.

As I was walking, I passed the sexual-health clinic, and I thought—like when you've gone to Topshop for a shirt and you think, *I may as well pick up some leggings while I'm here*— that I might as well pop into the sexual-health clinic, as it didn't look that busy, and have a general checkup. And then, like in a film, but with no one there to see it—why do the most ridiculous and unexpected things happen when you're alone?—as I opened the door to the clinic, an ex-boyfriend walked out (one of the six- to nine-monthers) with his arm round a crying girl who was obviously his girlfriend. I hadn't seen him for years. He and I went white.

"Oh, hello, snookums," he spluttered. Snookums? We'd never called each other *snookums* in our lives. Wasn't *snookums* something that people called each other on TV but that never happened in real life, like when women are called Michaela? Even I, with my paradigm of pet names, had never stooped so low.

"Hello!" I said. I nearly said, "What are you doing here?" but I remembered where we were, and that she was crying. At least I hadn't said, "Do you come here often?" He didn't introduce us. There was a silence, which I'm bad at dealing with, so I blurted out, "I've just had acid put on a wart on my forehead!" I lifted up my hair—which was still blowing around because we were half in the doorway and half out—to show them. They didn't look too impressed. I suddenly worried that she had some warty thing, too, but maybe down below, and that maybe, as she and I were custard cousins,* it was he who was the spreader.

---

*We have a saying in Matlock called "custard cousins"—I don't know if you have it where you're from. Custard cousins, as I'm sure you can guess, means that you've both had sex with the same person. Sometimes, especially if you work in the comedy industry in any capacity, you meet one of your custard cousins and you don't even know it. All these invisible connections running between us. Once you're custard cousins, you're always custard cousins. Make friends, make friends, never never break friends. Like they say in the Mafia.

"Bye!" I trilled and hurried away, my hand over the wart in case it fell off then and there, adding to the awkwardness of the situation.

A few days later the wart had turned a browny black, although the very most tips of it were still white, like it was trying hard to remain a little cauliflower. I was walking along with another comedian after a rehearsal. My hair behaved when I was inside, but now that we were out on the street, the shrively little cauliflower was exposed to all and sundry. He looked at me sideways as I was talking and said, "Ooh, you've got a little beetle on your head! Er—that must mean good luck!" Of course it must, mustn't it, because it would be such shit luck to just have a beetle crawling across your head without it meaning anything. "Hey, don't worry about that magpie stealing the engagement ring you were about to propose with—it means that when you buy another one, she'll definitely say yes!"

"No, it's not a beetle," I said to him. "It's a wart. But it's going to fall off in the next day, I reckon. I can feel it loosening, but I'm not allowed to pull it, or eat any Rice Krispies, just in case."

The next night I was gigging in a theater in Porthcawl, which is in Wales. There was a nice guy in a wheelchair at this gig who always sat in the front row and who was famous among comics because no matter how bad a gig you were having, he would always laugh. This night I was having such a horrible gig that even he was looking at the floor, and there was a guy who was heckling me for being English. I finished on the pedophile song, and as I yodeled the last line—"Pe-do-lae-do-lae-do-lae-do-lae-do-lae-do-lo-phile"—the wart fell off. I picked it up really quickly and scurried offstage. Next there was a break, and then the MC took the wart on in a sherry glass and tried to auction it off.

I WAS shaken out of my memory of the wart by the small guy in the tracksuit moving away from the bar and approaching us at the pool table. We three and the soldiers were still playing, and it was something of a league now. *He's talking to himself, like the old man*, I thought as he got closer. It was only when he drew up to the table that I realized he was rapping in a West Country accent. I'd never heard anyone rap in a West Country accent before. He was rapping about life in Plymouth. We were all quite enthralled, and as a result I was the only one who noticed him moving his cuff down over his hand and "hoovering up" all the pound coins that we had put down on the edge of the table for future games. He probably got about eight quid. He hadn't really wanted to tell us all about when he worked at the gift shop in the National Marine Aquarium or when he stole a lizard from Dartmoor Zoo by luring it with a hula hoop (which felt like it couldn't realistically happen)—it had all been a distraction technique. The rapper then disappeared toward the bar quickly, not even telling us whether the lizard was able to survive on leaves and instant noodles, and I was torn about whether to say anything. He probably wasn't making much of a living from music.

My instinct to protect him was irrelevant, as a few of the soldiers now noticed that their pound coins were gone and deduced what had happened. Then, as much as it could around a pool table, a massive fight broke out, like something from a Western. The cues were involved. Luckily, because we were all drunk, the soldiers were also fighting among themselves rather than all setting onto the rapper. Mickey, Ross, and I flattened ourselves against the wall. The girlfriends of the soldiers lackadaisically got up from the laps of their respective men and clustered in the corner, not even bothering to look at the action. I couldn't believe how blasé they were. I am simultaneously fascinated and horrified by fights, and even remember at school finding that raw desire to hurt another person quite hard to stomach. In my drunken state I kept trying to stop the fight, shouting things like, "He didn't mean it!" (of course he did) and "Eight quid! He probably wanted to buy the lizard some chips!" The fight didn't last very long, as the barman intervened, but it ended with the soldiers getting their pound coins back and telling the rapper not to come near the pool table.

Banned from the pool table area, the guy brooded by the bar as we recommenced our pool game as best we could—cues had been damaged and balls scattered everywhere. He kept coming near the table, then mock–leaping back as if he'd had an electric shock. Then, as we all watched, he walked straight over to the old man with the shopping bag, who'd fallen asleep. He took the shopping bag off the floor by the old man's feet, then prodded him on the arm. The old man woke up, very confused, and the rapper managed to sell the contents of the bag to him, picking out each item individually. The old man refused to pay anything for the book, but the rapper chucked it in for free. I wanted to defend my toothless friend the old man, but I didn't know what the rapper was capable of. Maybe he really did have a lizard in his pocket. Luckily the barman, who knew the old guy, had had enough, so the police were called. I reckon it was about five in the morning by this point, and I could barely stand. After the police came down and gave the old guy back his money and belongings, all of us decided to try to get some sleep, and stumbled out into the dawn. We exchanged details with the soldiers and their girlfriends, and then went back to our little B and B. Everything that could have happened in that little bar had happened. The idea of going to Plymouth for sex was now laughable. I didn't need sex! I had six new pen pals and was going to send them glow-in-the-dark erasers!

12

Isy discovers making lists
doesn't solve anything

Yet again, I had that weighty type of hangover where, despite copious amounts of water and tea, your mouth feels like you've just gobbled down ten dry Weetabixes. My mood was lightened when I walked into the kitchen and observed a cheerful Sue making chili con carne to take to a "lunch party" she was going to the following day. I hadn't ever heard of a lunch party; I secretly suspected she'd made up the term. It couldn't be like a dinner party but in the day, because you didn't normally take your own food to a dinner party, did you? She told me it was something she and her university friends did— each taking a dish to share. One of them only ever brought a bag of candy arranged on a doily and then tucked in with relish to all the other dishes. It was the same bloke who never bought a round. Of course it fucking was. It would be the same bloke who, in five years, would point out that he hadn't had any peas so owed 25p less than everyone else on the restaurant bill, the one who would ultimately try to negotiate the inclusion of lightbulbs and garden gnomes upon buying a house. Sue called her university friends her "unirellies"—an unnerving hybrid of *university* and *relation*.

No parties I went to, whether with unirellies or the usual myriad of misfits, involved people bringing food, but I thought it important to "sample" it and assuage my aching need for meat. Sue and I were so different. She wanted a boyfriend, but she couldn't find someone quite right. She had so many boxes for them to tick that she couldn't remember them all, even though she herself had devised them, based on a utopian vision of her future. I thought her standards were too high, but in really unusual ways: "He's wearing tan shoes, so that means he's a mummy's boy." This would be based on the fact that she'd once known a man with tan shoes who happened to be a mummy's boy. Surely there were other variables as well as the tan shoes. Calling his mum *mummy* although he was thirty-two, for example? "No, no, the tan shoes are enough evidence on their own."

I'd been spending more time with Sue over the last few months, as Amy and Gavin always seemed to be out at pregnancy classes, workshops, gatherings, or sporting escapades—which I'd started to refer to as "fun runs." On weekend mornings I'd lie in bed and think about how lucky I was not to have to run or go to some mutual meditation—type class, and then I'd stumble downstairs to the newsagent and buy trashy magazines and then get back in bed and eat fruit cocktail straight from the tin. Amy, Gavin, and I were like ships that passed in the early evening—me on my way to a gig or a night out; them, exhausted, back from some trip or other.

They traipsed in as Sue and I were mopping up the last of our chili with white bread and butter. I knew that something was wrong immediately, because (a) neither of them would meet my eye as I ate a bowl of cornflakes for dessert, and (b) they were carrying loads of those massive checkered bags from the discount shop.

When they'd put the bags in their bedroom, they came into the kitchen and stood together in front of the sink, as if I might try to drown myself when I heard what they were about to say, and Amy went, "We've got something to tell you."

Not again. Surely they couldn't be having another baby already? I didn't know much about how pregnancy worked. Maybe if you carried on having sex, another one could sneak in like a stowaway and be born a few months after the first. I didn't think this was possible, but it was genuinely the first thing that occurred to me. Or maybe they'd decided to split up. Amy, Sue, and I could bring up the baby in Camberwell. It would have three mums and eat crispy cornflake cakes morning, noon, and night. All three of us would. I started to get quite excited. We'd all sleep in the hall, passing chocolate biscuits around, taking it in turns to do feedings and tell ghost stories. We'd be fine. My mum, who used to be a midwife (or so she says), had once told me that babies could sleep in a shoebox—they just needed blankets and straw. No, not straw. Food.

Then, bravely holding hands with Amy and looking me

in the eye, Gavin said the next bit. "We're moving to a village near Bristol. We didn't know how to tell you."

To be honest, I had been ignoring the warning signs. Things had changed since New Year's. I'd sometimes come into the living room and see them guiltily and hastily closing what looked like a real-estate website on their laptop, and I'd once overheard Gav saying on the phone, "Well, we like the look of the Cotswolds." But I'd dismissed it. Everyone likes the look of the Cotswolds. It's like saying, "We like the look of Niagara Falls," or my saying, "Hey, I like the look of James Franco." And of course there would be advantages to their being in the countryside. They could probably have a garden, which is mere folklore in London, and they could probably leave their back door unlocked, and the baby would grow up understanding how to communicate with chickens and how to make that whistling noise when you blow through grass, and it would have a blackberry stain constantly round its mouth like a purple beard. I just couldn't believe they were going.

I said nothing, because I thought I might cry—it didn't help that I'd had three hours' sleep and was still slightly drunk. I didn't want them to feel bad, because it was completely their decision, and an understandable one at that, so I went over to the sink and started doing the dishes and just didn't say anything. It was so out of character for me to do the dishes apropos of nothing that there was a tense silence. Then Amy hugged me and said, "We'll really miss you. And you can come and visit all the time."

I'd never felt a bigger gulf between us. There was going

to be no shoebox and no chocolate biscuits. The fact that we'd started to refer to the baby as The Heir—although what it'd be inheriting apart from a lovely ginger beard and Amy's penchant for Pinot Grigio was unclear—would become a distant, silly memory as they cracked open elderflower cordial with other country parents. I felt like any of my mates' having a baby was as boring as any of my mates' getting married, but more permanent. I felt like they viewed me as stupid and immature, with my "let's have adventures" rule, like one day I might grow up and join their club. Only then would I know the Masonic handshake and be able to sympathize, and advise, and be their best mate again. Yet what I was doing— going out and living my life, not thinking about where things might lead—genuinely did feel right. I'd come out of a long-term relationship not that long ago that had been rotten for ages. Why was it so bizarre to everyone that I might actually be happy single? More important, why did I care what they thought?

That evening, the four of us sat down and ate together for the first time in ages. I was usually out, but I was too spent from the night before. I was in that soporific state where you've got the last dregs of being drunk and of memories from the night before, you've done nothing of any value because of the hangover, it's now dark, and you're going to eat more chili and drink Jack and Cokes. Yes, Sue had made so much chili that we had it again that night. We all avoided the fact that Amy and Gavin were moving out. All day I'd been half aware of them having discussions about e-mailing real-estate agents and the plural of "man with van"; "men with ven."

After the chili, Sue made Eton mess, and then we all devised a game to do with word association that involved being fed Eton mess at a very rapid rate by two other parties at the same time. On the surface, nothing was wrong at all. I was actually going to call it a night when Gavin, a bit drunk now, said, "By this time next year we'll have a baby!"

"I know, mate," replied Sue, shaking her head. She'd had a lot of beer and had acquired a distinctive Weeble-like quality to her balance. "Maybe by this time next year, Isy and I will have a boyfriend!"

"The same one?" I said. "It'll save on rent."

"Come on," she said, "let's write a list of what we want in men. I've been meaning to do it for ages."

"Why?" I said. "I'm actively not seeking one."

"This'll help you!" said Amy. "So you can reject them more readily, 'cos they don't meet the requirements."

The only real reason I agreed is that I love making lists. I love ticking boxes and closing the book, turning the light off and knowing I've done enough for the day.

On my tenth birthday I was given a big writing pad, and I proceeded to write the word *please* on every line. That was all I wrote—the word *please* again and again. Then I got to the end of the one hundred pages and that was all I had, and I didn't know why I'd done it. What was the one thing I wanted to change? I had so much power at my fingertips! At that time, all ten-year-olds, like me, wore White Musk perfume oil from the Body Shop and Sweater Shop tops and were dead against testing cosmetics on animals. Whenever you went down any city high street, there would be stalls about animal testing with really sad photos of rabbits with shampoo in their eyes. So I wrote, on the very last line, "stop testing cosmetics on animals." I underlined the word *stop* just for good measure. I ripped all the pages out of the pad and put them into an envelope, and I didn't know who to send it to, so I sent it to the Queen. I suppose my logic was that she was the leader of the country and could stop anything. I never received a reply. Maybe I'd send this list to the Queen, too, and then she could reserve a guy for me, and let him loose in Camberwell in about eight months for me to stumble across outside the pub in the shopping mall, or in the sexual-health clinic.

Sue's list was, as I'd expected, very detailed. It said things like:

> Listens when I speak and doesn't just say "mmm" and nod head
> Never comments on other women's appearances, good or bad
> Doesn't talk about self in third person when drunk

I watched her large, farmerlike hands that I loved so much scribbling furiously at the kitchen table as I chomped on meaty hunks of meringue. Gavin had already contested number two, the point about women's appearances. Wouldn't Sue want her boyfriend to say her mum looked nice on their wedding day?

"You know what I mean!" Sue spat good-naturedly, swigging deep brown home brew that even I wouldn't touch that her brother had brought round from his "laboratory" in Somerset. After she'd finished her list, it was my turn. I wrote:

Rarely mixes up *you're* and *your*

Rarely uses moisturizer (if does, uses mine)

Is kind

Can laugh at self

Doesn't call my mum Val, which my ex did, which isn't her name

Abides, but doesn't really care for, dogs, horses, farmers' markets, and the sea

Doesn't like Shredded Wheat, apart from when it's covered in chocolate

Knows how to build dry stone walls and fires (not imperative)

Tans easily but doesn't burn

Quick reader

Doesn't like camping

Doesn't want to move to countryside (racists and Agas*)

Gavin read my list through. "A lot of these seem to be negatives," he said. "Doesn't like Shredded Wheat. Doesn't like camping. Maybe that's why you're not meeting anyone."

"OK, two things," I answered, realizing I was a bit more tipsy than I'd previously thought. "(a), I meet people all the time. You know I do. You know I don't want a boyfriend. So why do you think I have to get one? It's like you think I'm a kid who doesn't know any better. She's"—I jerked my thumb toward Sue—"the one who wants one. And (b), that list isn't serious anyway. It's only a stupid game."

---

*Aga cast-iron stoves, a staple of country homes. Along with cold bathrooms, stray jigsaw pieces, and strange rituals involving weeding and crossword puzzles.

"Bits of it are serious, Is," said Amy gravely. I normally love it when people call me "Is," but this grated on me even more. "You've been saying the moisturizer and 'your versus you're' thing since college."

"If you knew me at all," I shouted, "you'd see that I've softened each of those points due to the constant ineptitude of noughties men." I was quite impressed that I'd used the word *ineptitude* in what was rapidly becoming an argument.

"OK, not serious?" said Gav, taking the list from Amy. I couldn't believe this was happening over a stupid game. "Doesn't want to move to countryside? Racists and a gas? What gas?" They hadn't even read it properly.

"The gas from the racists' arses!" I shouted, getting up. "The racists who will become your best friends!"

I walked out of the room and slammed the front door. Then returned for my Oyster card, wallet, and keys. Then left properly. I needed to be as far away from ultrasounds, iron tablets, and hypnobirthing CDs as possible. It had been too long. I was going to see Ben.

13

Isy and an Australian scream questions at strangers

Everyone, by the age of thirty, should have a provisional driver's license, the ability to cook one dish well, and someone they can call at any time if they want to have sex. I had one thing from this list of three. I'd lost my provisional, and I still couldn't cook—unless you counted the "fry-up pie." But I had someone to call up. He was called Ben and he was from Australia and was a few years younger than me. He was just fun, like patting a donkey is sometimes fun. He lived in Australia a lot of the time, and I hadn't seen him for ages. He wasn't meant to be a nucleus in anyone's life but his own, and that suited me fine at this moment.

I met Ben when I was doing a fringe play at a tiny pub theater, just after I graduated. "Fringe play" means you're not getting paid, or not paid much, but you try to get agents to come watch you, and if they won't, which they mainly don't, you just try to have fun. My strongest memory about this show is that the dressing room didn't have a toilet and one night I was backstage, the show had started, and I realized I was absolutely bursting for a wee. It was at that terrible stage where you know that if you move even an inch, there's a risk of leakage. It *hurt*. I knew I had time to go, as the other actress, Charlie, was onstage doing a long song and then I was due on to sing a song about Connex South Eastern, the train company. Unable to think of any other solution, I opened the window of the dressing room, scuttled onto the roof of the pub, and—hallelujah!—released my bladder onto the unsuspecting ants in the gutter below my spread-eagled thighs. Meanwhile, onstage, Charlie forgot the words to her song, skipped a section, and jumped to the last verse, thus shaving approximately a minute off the overall time. I suddenly heard urgent whispers of, "Isy! Isy! We're on!" rising to "ISSSSSYYYYYY!" from an actor who'd been acting as a watchman for anyone spying on me because he was gay and therefore immune to my vaginal prowess.

I was at that stage of release where there's no going back, where you're thinking, "Wow, it's actually worth getting to this level of pain for this sweet, sweet feeling," like when you think you've lost your keys and then you find them and the relief is so great that you fleetingly consider employing someone to hide them in a peculiar place every few months so you can have the buzz of finding them.

"ISSSSSYYYYY!" I could hear my Connex South Eastern introductory music starting, which was only about eight bars. I didn't have long. Against every bodily instinct, I gritted my teeth and clenched my pelvic floor muscles. In about five seconds, I leapt back through the open window into the dressing room, pulling my—I distinctly remember this—red knickers, which were really on their last legs, up with my trousers, and ran straight onto the stage. As I did the Connex South Eastern song, I could have sworn that my trousers were getting wetter and wetter, that I hadn't been able to stop. My body was one step behind—or ahead of—my mind, and conscience, and pride. I could actually feel warmth on the insides of my legs, and I couldn't believe that the audience, whose faces I could see clearly in the small room, wasn't staring and pointing. When I got back into the dressing room, I looked down—to see nothing at all. I'd stopped as I'd jumped through the window. It was just the adrenaline that convinced me that my legs were wet. Strangely, I felt slightly disappointed—but I needn't have worried. This was just the beginning of the adventure.

Ben worked behind the bar at the pub, and we'd never spoken to each other, just exchanged smiles as I rushed up the stairs to make my call time or as the rest of the cast and I sank pints postshow, often with the seven or so people who'd made up our audience. The night of the pants incident, my agent, Franco, was in, watching. Franco was from Italy and couldn't speak very good English at all. He ran his agency from an office that looked like it also served as his bedsit, and that I'd paid to join. This is a complete no-no—we were always told at drama school never to pay to join an agency—but I'd been completely desperate. At our acting showcase I'd had no agent interest at all—it probably hadn't helped that I'd done a monologue that I'd thought was about a flashlight and didn't understand was about masturbation until weeks afterward—and I left college representing myself. I'd get the actors' newspaper, *PCR—Production and Casting Report*, and, like many other actors in my position, apply for every job I was suitable for and many that I wasn't. I also sent about fifty CVs a week to agencies, and then we'd put the most blunt rejection letters on our kitchen wall and circle any particularly dismissive or misspelled bits, draw cocks and balls on them, and so on.

Franco was the only one who'd replied saying we should meet, and I hadn't realized then that I would have to pay. I went to his office and performed two monologues for him, which is something I've never heard of another agent asking for in my life. I did Hermia from *A Midsummer Night's Dream* and then the good old "flashlight" one. After I finished, he asked me which one had been the Shakespeare. When he revealed that he was joking, I was so relieved I signed up on the spot. He'd ring me up about once a month and shout, "Isobel! You have audition!"

"Franco—great!" I'd reply. "Where?"

"Isobel!" he'd yell. "Don't ask me too many question!" Then he'd slam the phone down and ring me back five minutes later and say, "King Cross! Unpaid student film about abortion! Take tap shoes!"

It was obvious that Franco hadn't "gotten" the play, but he kept nodding and saying, "Bright scenery, bright scenery," which is nearly as bad as saying to an actor, "How did you learn all those lines?" He shot off pretty pronto, promising to call me about more "audition!" and I was with the rest of the cast when I noticed Ben again and thought, *Sod it. I've nearly pissed myself onstage tonight. Having my agent as an agent's worse than having no agent at all. What have I got to lose?*

Pinned to the wall near the door of the pub was a piece of gray cardboard with the actors' photos and names on it, just in case any Hollywood producers had to slip out early and wanted to make a note of which actress it was who'd bolted onto the stage looking like she was about to piss herself. I took mine down, wrote my phone number on the back, rolled it up like a degree scroll, and got into the queue at the bar. It was quite busy, and it took ages to get to the front. When I did, a girl tried to serve me. She said, "What can I get you?" I didn't know what to do—I didn't want to say, "Give this to him" (I didn't know his name) or "I want to be served by him"—so I just gazed at the drip trays in silence and slowly went cross-eyed, and after a few moments she went away. When I could sense that she'd gone, I made my eyes go normal again and looked up. Ben was moving a bottle of crusty Advocaat. I thrust the "scroll" over the bar and into his hands and then scurried back to my fellow actors and told them, too, then giddily downed the rest of my pint and scarpered out the door. That night he texted me and we met up a few times afterward, and from then on, although years went by, we'd had a little arrangement that might pick itself up between any respective relationships, although neither of us thought of it like that. I guess that's the beauty of such arrangements. If they really are arrangements, they're like bubbles you shouldn't try to touch, or they'll pop and you'll wonder if there ever was an arrangement. Trust in the arrangement. Look at the rainbow of colors in the arrangement. Leave the bloody arrangement alone, for God's sake. Arrangement arrangement arrangement.

I wanted to go to his in Clapham, but he had "a shitload of Aussies on the living-room floor—it's like a budget Foster's advert," so after we had a couple of drinks in the pub, he came back to mine. My housemates, I was pleased to observe, were in bed. The list was gone.

"That phone-number-on-the-back-of-the-photo thing was so awesome!" Ben said, like he always did. We were sitting on the roof: although our flat was pretty basic, the landlord had somehow wangled possession of the roof of the entire row of flats, which was about the length of five houses and covered in defunct chimneys. The view was of a Chinese restaurant, a pub, and a main road, but if you closed your eyes, just for a moment you could pretend you were anywhere else in London that was near a Chinese restaurant, a pub, and a main road. Once, back in the good old days, Amy, Gav, a couple of mates, and I had been up there drinking, and we started playing a game. First we would shout, "Oy!" to passersby. They would never guess that we were three stories above them, and it would take ages for them to register where the noise was coming from. When they finally discovered us, we shouted a question like, "What's the capital of Iceland?" That's always the first question that springs to mind when people ask me to ask them a question. Always, in any situation. People mostly know the answer, and these guys did, so we threw them a Refresher bar and an unwanted baked potato. We were going to chuck them a couple of cans of lager, but that would have been dangerous. We did it for ages that night with different passersby. The roof was a great place.

Ben and I were the only ones up there tonight. I hadn't seen him for years, and he'd stopped doing bar work and done a bit of film writing, then stopped that and started a PhD, then stopped that, and was now buying bikes from eBay, doing them up, and selling them on.

"It's great," he said. "I get to meet lots of different kinds of people." It sounded like something you'd write to your French pen pal—a slightly inauthentic sentence whose only function was to use up vocabulary. "I have brown hair. I like swimming. I eat cheese on Mondays." But perhaps he meant it. He was really into people's stories, in a big way. He could meet someone and spend hours talking to them about something that happened with a hookah pipe in Morocco or how they slept on Bondi Beach for years. He showed me with glee a little tattoo he'd had done on his arm. It was lots of Chinese lettering and lines.

"What does it mean?" I asked, feeling the question to be obligatory. I'd love for someone to show me their Chinese tattoo one day, one that covers their whole body, including their face, and for me to just go, "Hm," and not ask what it meant.

"It took ages," Ben said. "It's a translation of the English barcode for Fairy liquid.* They're all Chinese numbers." He rubbed his hands with glee. "They look like letters, don't they?"

"Yeah!" I said.

"Fooled everyone!"

---

* Fairy liquid is a brand of dishwashing liquid that makes your hands as soft as can be. I am not sponsored by Fairy liquid. Nor, despite appearances, was Ben.

WE LOOKED out over the line of chimneys into the smoggy night, sipping from warm cans of lager. "My mind's too active for me to have one job," Ben told me. He'd accepted that he'd have periods of living with his parents as he worked out what he really wanted to do. He wanted to start his own business making T-shirts, but he wasn't sure which kind, or his own business repairing bikes.

"Well, you kind of do that anyway," I said. "It's great."

"Yeah . . ." he said vaguely. "Yeah."

He made a joint. I told him about Amy and Gavin, who were asleep below us, and how I felt about everything that was happening.

"Jeeeeez," he said, blowing out smoke toward the Chinese restaurant. "What losers. When I think my life's shit, when I'm in my old room at my parents', in my single bed, playing my PlayStation, and I'm too stoned to go to the kitchen and get an ice-cream cake, I'll remember that my life could be worse. I could have kids, or be a fucking homeowner, part of the system, a servant to The Man."

"Yeah," I said. "What's an ice-cream cake?"

"Ice cream," he said. "In a cake."

Suddenly I wanted to play the game where we shouted questions to people. Ben said it sounded great. We went to the edge of the roof, stopping to run around a few chimneys like in *Mary Poppins*, and shouted down to some people who were smoking outside the pub.

"Hey!" shouted Ben. One of them looked across the road and then back toward his mates.

"Let's shout 'hey' after three!" I said.

Ben and I giggled at top volume in unison, "One two three, hey after three!" This time two of them looked, and saw us.

Ben shouted, "What am I thinking about right now?" He'd gone off piste. They were meant to be yes/no questions, hard as you like but with a definite right answer that contestants on *Eggheads* would know. There was silence from the group. One of them dropped a lighter and picked it up, then they went back to chatting.

Ben shouted louder, "What's the meaning of life?"

The original guy looked up at us and shouted, "Well, it's not standing on roofs shouting stuff!" The group dissolved into laughter.

Ben tried again. "Who would win a fight between an octopus with two legs and a jellyfish with a veering problem?" The lads went back inside the pub.

"Come on," I said, "let's go and eat some chili."

"Why wouldn't someone answer that?" he chuckled as we went through the tiny roof door and down the little stairs to the flat. "I thought of that ages ago, when I was in Thailand. It's, like, lodged in my brain, and it comes out whenever I'm stoned. It'd be my *Mastermind* topic. Who'd win a fight between an octopus with two legs and a jellyfish with a veering problem. They wouldn't know what the fuck to do if I came out with that. Would they?" I looked at him. His eyes were wide and very blue.

"No," I giggled firmly, taking the chili out of the fridge. "No, they wouldn't."

14

Isy tests her new hair theory

Sue and I gripped hands as we waved Amy, Gavin, and Mark off. I hadn't seen Mark since New Year's, and now we were well into spring. They'd managed to cram most of the bags and suitcases into good old Keith for the journey to Amy and Gavin's new home in the village near Bristol. The trunk was tied down with weak-looking string, and I could spy Gav's guitar case and Amy's old tax returns in the darkness within. All the rest of their stuff was piled up in the living room, and Mark was coming back to get it the next day while Amy and Gavin settled in. I smiled at the familiar dents in Keith as they pulled out. Then suddenly Sue and I were in the kitchen and I was putting the kettle on and Keith was probably already stuck in traffic in Vauxhall and I was thinking, *Did they just go?* in the same way as I sometimes get out of the shower and put a towel on and think, *Did I just have a shower? I hope so.*

I'd imagined the moment of them going so many times. I'd felt sure I was going to have a hollow feeling for days. But actually, I felt kind of detached. I had a bit of writing to do, and then I was going back to Matlock to see my parents. The only thing that was different from how I'd imagined us waving them off was that Sue had a new boyfriend, Al. They were at that stage where everything the other one does, even breathing or moving something absentmindedly, seems magical, like only they could do it in that particular way. "The lid would never have been left off the biscuit jar if it hadn't been for him!" He'd stood there alongside us as we'd seen Amy and Gavin off, ignoring the fact that Sue and I were holding hands, waving his own hand vaguely so as not to be impolite, but not definitely enough to guarantee that he was waving at *them*. He didn't want to impose. I thought that was very gallant. And he loved the 1980s herb parsley like she did; and had dark, bushy hair so thick it didn't seem to be made of individual hairs, instead comprising one large mass, like a miniature country, and bigger hands than she did, which was tough to achieve.

I was on the train to Matlock, safely ensconced in a soft cocoon of Twix and Anne Tyler, when Ben texted. "Wanna play?" We never put kisses. It was so much easier.

"Soz," I replied. "On way to Matlock. Amy and Gavin left today. Feeling bit weird now."

What I loved about our arrangement is that it felt more honest and meaningful than the spluttery start of most relationships, when at any given time, each party is trying to gauge how the other feels—whether they should put a kiss at the end of a text; chastising themselves when they've put a full stop at the end of a sentence, as the proceeding kiss has gone into uppercase and they're still at the lowercase stage; that awful "chat" that sometimes arises, where phrases like "*seeing* each other" and "I'm bad with relationships" and "Um, biscuit?" are bandied around.

I detest the word *slag*, because it implies damaged goods, a loss of control—or, worse, a very large sense of control, almost destiny: that the woman somehow "set out" to just sleep with as many men as possible in her stupid, worthless life. It's up to anyone who they sleep with. I think there's something in respecting yourself, and that's harder to negotiate your way through when you're younger, but if you don't respect yourself, and you try to garner love or attention through putting out—perhaps not being wholly bothered who with—that shouldn't invite shame or ridicule. It's sad, and, more important, it can change. Confidence is key in so many things, it's flabbergasting. Sex can be so great, and so terrible, and I think sometimes people make the mistake of thinking they will always get attached if they do it, and then it becomes a bit Pavlovian. I enjoyed having sex with him—do I want to marry him? No! You can enjoy having sex with him and you can be eating a Peperami in a car on your own literally two minutes later, the wind screaming into your face, your eyes streaming because of it, on your way to buy an extra-large popcorn and watch an amazing Japanese animation film on your own at the cinema. You can enjoy having sex with him and it can have as much importance and weight as a conversation with your mum about whether sweet potato is one of your five a day. It's up to you.

Arrangements, by their very nature, are delicate. I could have fallen for Ben as he deftly pawed my bum, or he could have fallen for me as I charmingly sidestepped the dastardly hand-job yet again, but that was what made it kind of precious. And you're not a slag when you're making them proper coffee in the morning, your head bobbing along to the Chemical Brothers, cheeks pink, a sweaty sheet clasped around your naked body with one hand like you're a joyful little caterpillar. You're not a slag when you've carved up fresh pineapple and presented it to them balanced on a hardback copy of *The Vibe History of Hip Hop*. Then it's like a French film—till you put on trackie bottoms and politely ask them to leave because you're doing a *Simpsons* marathon. Then it's better than any film. The good thing is, you don't make plans. Stuff just happens.

His reply came back. "No worries babe." I hugged my arms and looked out the window. I could see my weary reflection in the thick glass. "I'll be OK about A and G," I wrote, dithered, then deleted.

THAT EVENING as I walked the ten-minute journey from the small train station to my parents' house, I greeted three lads from my year at school. I realized with mild horror and then amusement that I still thought of everyone in "school years." Even though I left school in the mid-nineties, when I meet any new person I work out how many years above or below me they were at school, and I imagine having known them at school, and them ignoring me in the common room because they were in the upper sixth and I was just a measly old fifth-year with my scruffy backpack and Doc Martens with EMF and Simply Red written on them in correction fluid and that a school friend of mine had cut the soles more or less off with garden shears one night, making walking virtually impossible.

It dawned upon me that I'd always secretly thought I'd end up with a lad from Matlock, or Belper if I must, and move back home to have kids, who would talk with the same accent as me. I didn't factor in the fact that most of my work would require me to be in London, and that I'd put roots down there. I'd pictured myself eventually settling down with some swarthy guy from school, perhaps from a local farming family but who went away to a good university and has now returned, who I bump into at the Boat one Christmas. His wife has died young, he tells me, and he has a little daughter, who I'm *amazing* with, and I learn to feed lambs and rear sheep and live back among my brethren, frying sausages without having to cut them in half to see if there's any pink—just *knowing* they're done—and I start to look beautiful without makeup, and know the area so well that I'm able to give directions to locals without looking at my phone. Although he's from a farming family, he hates dogs and early mornings, and he never kills any of the farm animals. Children come and feed them grain, whatever that is, which I divide into plastic bags and sell for 50p, along with misshapen floury scones. Inland Revenue let us off paying tax because we live by the laws of the land and are good people, and because he has an uncle in the Sheffield office, and there's a pool table in the basement.

Of the three men I saw in Matlock this evening (I supposed, after all, that they *were* men now), one had his son with him, face covered in what looked like peanut butter; one was with his wife, who hadn't been at school with us; and the third was hammered. Despite these differences, they had a few things in common. Each of them had gained a few pounds, and all three of them looked like their heads had grown through their hair. It didn't look to me like they were losing their hair; I couldn't accept that. To me, it looked like the hair had stubbornly remained at the same height as always and their skulls had just spurted through it and now there was no hair to cover the skin that had grown through.

I told this to my mum when I got through the door.

"Mmmm," she said. "You can dress it up how you want. They're losing their hair. They're older. So are you."

"So are *you*, mate!" I yelled, running upstairs to the sanctuary of my old bedroom and slamming the door. Safety at last.

15

Isy and Jo's Dating Agency

My old Matlock bedroom is a time capsule. When I was about fourteen I painted a horizontal line along every wall, encompassing everything in its path: wastebin, chest of drawers, shelves, wardrobe, radiator. I painted everything above the line, including the wall, bright pink; everything below it bright orange; and the ceiling bright purple. When you were in there it was like you were going slowly insane, like something that would have taken place in *A Clockwork Orange*. I'd gotten used to it by now, though. Before I'd done the painting, I'd taken all my posters down and afterward put them back up in the same places, so they were the only items that had escaped the paintbrush. They were all still on the walls: Carter USM, James, Jesus Jones, EMF, the Levellers. In an orange drawer were Take That and New Kids on the Block posters, relegated to make room for indie bands. I took them out and looked through them. On each New Kids poster, Joey McIntyre's mouth had disappeared because of me and my mates practicing snogging on it. There was just a rather grim hole where it should have been. If he'd had his hands up to the sides of his face, it would have looked like a pop version of *The Scream*. I looked at Take That. I was one of the original Take That fans: I'd seen them before most of the country had. When I was about eleven or twelve, Take That came to play at the Matlock Bath Illuminations road show, and I went with my best mate, Jo. We didn't know anything about Take That— we'd found a flyer on a car in Nottingham and they were all wearing black leather and that was enough for us. We'd never seen black leather for real.

That Sunday at seven o'clock sharp, there we were in the front row of a crowd of about thirty people, most of whom were under three or over seventy, all of us clustered around an outdoor bandstand in the Pavilion Gardens. The only other band I'd ever seen live was the Christian youth band Matthew, Mark, Luke, and Darren,* and it was a big step for me to see a live dance group in squeaky trousers and baby oil, leaping onto the rickety bandstand with oodles of energy, singing words like *girl* and *baby* and *oooh*. It's only now that I get how hard they must have been working, traveling the country to schools and charity fetes and workingmen's clubs night after night, to get used to performing as a band and to try to drum up some buzz. I just assumed they loved Matlock. After a couple of fast numbers to get everyone going—and they did—a

---

*Among the four, the only real name was Darren. The day I found that out at thirteen, a bit of me died.

slower song came in on the backing track and one of the band stepped forward, scanning the crowd for a girl he could sing to. I had the kind of face that always got picked out of crowds. Not because I was beautiful, but because my face was so run-of-the-mill that everyone always assumed that I never got a go at getting picked out of crowds, and therefore I became the girl who always got picked out of crowds.

And yet again, my face was picked out. Howard Donald—the Gary Barlow of the group—fixed me in his gaze, leaned on the amp, which was balanced on some beer crates, and sang—just to me. I cried, he smiled, and everyone looked at both of us, but mostly at him. It was very intense for me, as you can imagine. As a very young teenager, to have a topless sweaty man sing just for you is not an everyday occurrence. I was wild with embarrassment and crippled by hormones. Everything was in Technicolor. Eventually the song ended, as all great songs must, and I felt that I had to do something to say thank-you. I didn't want to be just another mousy young girl he'd sung to—I was wise enough to know that he probably picked a different girl out at every gig, and tomorrow night in Leicester it'd be someone called Lesley with hoop earrings and black roots and an equally dry mouth. So as the music ended to applause, and the backing track came in with a more lively song, I reached into my pocket, pulled out a pound coin—which my dad had given me for lemonade and toffees—and threw it toward Howard Donald's head. He was looking across at Jason Orange and didn't see it. It flew through the air toward him and he happened to turn back to the front at exactly the right moment, and it hit him just above his left eye. He didn't look happy. I supposed that having anything thrown at your head when you're not expecting it is bad. Even having a wad of twenty-pound notes (my current fee for leaving the stage during a gig) or a marshmallow thrown at your head would be, at best, confusing until you realized what it was. I skulked toward the back of the crowd as the pound coin rolled toward the edge of the bandstand and settled next to the amps. Later, after everyone had left, I got Jo to go get it and we spent it on pinball in the arcades.

I looked in the next drawer and found loads of cassette tapes, including ones containing songs I'd written about boys. Not always boys I fancied. Sometimes boys other girls fancied, from their points of view. Basically, around the same time as the Take That pound-coin incident, Jo and I had set up a "dating agency" called Isy and Jo's Dating Agency. One of us had a rubber stamp kit where you could spell out any word, and most of our working days involved us stamping ISY AND JO'S DATING AGENCY onto everything we could find. Absolutely every swimming, ballet, and music certificate of mine pre–1992, including the one where they spelled my name "Isobel Shuttle," every recipe and address book belonging to my parents, every wooden surface in my then bedroom, has the dating agency stamp on it. I don't know if it was just misplaced advertising, or if we were trying to make out that all that stuff was now the property of the dating agency, like when a general takes over a tiny village.

We also stamped all our schoolbooks, and our forearms and calves every day, and sometimes our cheeks, and soon other girls started to take notice. "What does your dating agency do? Can it set me up with Kristian Schmid? Can it get me out of geography?" We explained that we didn't make dreams come true like that—we built up profiles for each client and matched them with the most suitable contender. A few girls signed up, but when we produced their matches, having dissected their looks and interests in line with some unsuspecting boys', our work was invariably met with responses like, "Ungh! Him? No way! I snogged him last year and he kept his teeth closed like a cage and said 'C-c-c-c-c-c' while we kissed! Give me my 20p back!" We hadn't even attempted to set them up. We'd fallen at the first hurdle.

Jo and I decided we needed to radically change the business if it was going to succeed. We needed a gimmick to pique our clients' interest. That's when we came up with the idea of writing love songs. I'd started playing the guitar and writing songs a couple of years before. At the time, my most popular song—among myself and Jo—was called "I've Had an Eventful Day," about a middle-aged man who had had a breakdown and lay in bed all day but then lied to people when they asked him what he'd been doing by saying he'd had an eventful day. I'd never tried to write a love song. But if Isy and Jo's Dating Agency was going to survive, it needed to take some risks. I would start writing tailor-made love songs, which we'd play to the boy in question, and as a result he would become convinced of the girl's love for him and would therefore fall immediately in love with her. Amazing.

We didn't concentrate on actually matching clients up anymore—that had been a rookie error—we were just hell-bent on landing whichever guy the girl wanted, regardless of who was batting out of whose league. The songs always began in the key of D and always contained the same chords: D, C, G, and A. The first song I wrote was a tester: it was from Jo's point of view, about a boy called Jack March, who was from a nearby village called Bonsall and went to a different school. I knew him, so I didn't find it hard to write. He was the kind of guy we were really into at the time: he had long dirty-blond hair, very straight and almost down to his bum, and quite small, almost feminine eyes; and he wore things like German army coats and paisley vests and of course the regular trope of Doc Martens, except that he didn't have EMF and certainly not Simply Red (had I gone temporarily insane?) graffitied upon them. We tried not to make it too soppy. It went:

> *Jack, Jack, Jack, Jack March*
> *Jack, Jack, Jack, Jack March.*
> *Jack March!*[*]
> *Jack, I really love your blond hair*
> *It's enough to make people stare*
> *Jack, I really hate it when you give me a glare*
> *Why can't we be a pair?*
> *Jack, I really love your blue eyes*
> *They're as blue as the bluest skies*
> *Jack, I really hate it when we have to say bye*
> *For you, I would die*
> *Jack, Jack, Jack, Jack March*
> *Jack March!*[†]

---

[*]Presumably in case he thought it could be about a different Jack.
[†]Presumably in case he'd forgotten that it wasn't about a different Jack.

Jack, I really love your Primark waistcoat
I guess we're in the same boat (spoken)
I'm a freak and so are you
And we both sniff glue
Jack, Jack, Jack, Jack March
Jack March!

The blue-eyes bit is very bad. I think I was just looking for a rhyme for *die*. Speaking of which, "For you, I would die" is a very bold statement to make to someone you've seen about six times at under-eighteen rock gigs and never spoken to. It also comes across as a bit needy. The Primark waistcoat thing was a joke. Jack didn't sniff glue, and the closest Jo and I had gotten to it was using a stick of it to apply glitter to our business cards, but I think this bit was supposed to be edgy.

The next thing to do was to work out how to get him to hear it. I taught it to her, but she didn't feel confident singing it on her own, so we decided to do it together. So he'd know who it was from, over the trusty D chord Jo and I said in unison, "A song for Jack March, from Jo Gibbs." Now on to how to get it to him, and whether live or recorded. We went through the various options. Go to his house, throw stones at his bedroom window, and serenade him? We decided against this, as he wouldn't be able to tell who we were in the dark, unless Jo shined a flashlight into her own face, which might look a bit creepy. If you opened your window in the night to see a dismembered head chanting, "A song for Jack March, from Jo Gibbs," you probably wouldn't immediately propose, which was of course the aim.

Another option was to set up a gig, invite him, and play it to him there. We were very much into live music and I was already in my first band, Isy Suttie and the Muppets. The only gig Isy Suttie and the Muppets had ever done was at Starkholmes Village Hall in a battle of the bands competition. I downed loads of beer before I went on and just played open strings because I'd forgotten all the chords. I then promptly ran onto the recreation ground behind the hall and vomited into a spiderweb and stumbled around for the rest of the night with the remainder of it draped around my head like tinsel. It wouldn't be difficult to teach "Jack March" to the members of the Muppets, but it might be a bit much for Jack for the song to be premiered in that environment. Saving face with his mates might muddy his decision of whether to marry Jo or not.

We decided that the best option was to record the song onto a cassette tape and somehow get it to him. That way, we didn't have to see his face while he listened to it, and he could keep it forever. I was sad about using a whole sixty-minute tape to record a two-minute song, so I decided to record a bonus track, which was my version of "(Everything I Do) I Do It for You" by Bryan Adams. There's a guitar solo in that song that precedes the line "Look into your heart, babe" and then continues afterward. There was no way I could even contemplate attempting it, so I strummed the chords underneath and sang the guitar solo. We stamped ISY AND JO'S DATING AGENCY on the inlay card, because the brand was always at the forefront of our minds, and we got a passport photo of Jo and taped it in. We didn't want to drop it through his door—although we knew where he lived, of course—in case his mum or dad found it, so we decided that the easiest option was to cut school, get the bus to his school in the nearby town of Wirksworth, find his schoolbag while he was in assembly, and put it in there.

Jo and I traveled on the bus to Anthony Gell School and managed to get in, no problem. His bag was a green backpack, but there were lots of green backpacks, so we panicked and handed it to the school receptionist, who promised to get it to Jack. The tape was delivered to Jack as promised, in class; he played it to *all his classmates and teacher*, and the next day the teacher then played the tape *in assembly* to demonstrate creativity. We heard all this from various kids who were at Jack's school. The teacher playing the tape was, in theory, a good person—we had an endorsement from an adult and advertising for the dating agency, and maybe we'd even get some clients from Wirksworth!—but everyone who heard it thought we were unhinged, including Jack, and he didn't get in touch; and when we went to the end of his road on a Saturday with water bombs to see if he wanted to come out and play with the water bombs, he sent his sister to tell us to go home.

Although Jack had failed to propose to Jo, she and I were pleased enough with the standard of the song itself to continue the dating agency. The girl who was commissioning a song would pay us however she could. We got strawberry sweets, erasers in the shape of teddy bears, bath pearls. Once we got a bird's nest someone's grandfather had woven with his bare hands. But no matter how hard we tried, and even with the introduction of the A seventh chord, none of the songs I wrote worked. If anything, they made the situation between the girl and boy worse, and some clients demanded their payments back. Jo and I came to the reluctant conclusion that only the person who's in love with the boy can write the song.

So I wrote a song about a boy called Sam Roe, and for the first time it was about a guy *I* fancied. It wasn't the Sam I'd broken up with at Christmas—what a lovely tale that would have been. No, it was Sam Roe. Sam Roe was, of course, best friends with Jack March. At the age of thirteen, you had to fancy someone who was best mates with the guy your best mate fancied. Sam was quite similar looking to Jack, with some small differences: he had brown hair and brown eyes, which were very large. He also wore a red bandanna all the time. I don't think he ever took it off. "Sam" started in D, of course, and went:

> *Sam, you are mega*
> *Not only that, you are funny and clever*
> *Sam, un deux trois quatre cinq six*
> *It doesn't matter that your hair is dripping with*
>   *grease*
> *Sam, you're a hippie*
> *But sometimes you go down to the chippie*
> *Sam, your hair is long and brown*
> *I think of you when I'm feeling down*
> *I think of you*
> *I think of you*
> *I think of you*
> *Woah*
> *Sam, your second name is R-O-E*
> *I love you, but you don't love me*

Sam, of love my heart is full
I love you so much, it's unbelievable
Sam, I love you and I hope you love me, too
I've loved you since I first saw you
Sam, I love you but I know you hate me
I'd love you even more if you would give me a
  Frenchie
Give me a Frenchie
Give me a Frenchie
Give me a Frenchie
Woah
SAM.

I don't know why I thought being a "hippie" precluded a visit to the chip shop—I'm not sure chips are high on the list with nuclear power and bombs—but a rhyme's a rhyme. Then it descends into misery. What was I thinking? You can't do yourself down to that extent and then command a Frenchie three times.

This time we did deliver a cassette tape of the song to his house—we didn't have to hide anymore, since the Jack March assembly debacle. I loved Sam Roe, and I didn't care if the butcher and the local pub landlord knew; I didn't care when everyone on Sam's lane gathered in their doorways, doors ajar, grubby children peeking round parents' trouser legs, all slowly shaking their heads as they watched Jo and me creep up Sam's driveway and drop the tape through his letterbox. And yet again, it didn't work. I don't think they even played it in assembly that time. We hung around Bonsall a bit in the weeks that followed, armed with water bombs and water pistols, unsure which aqua-based artillery Sam would favor, but we never even saw him. Eventually a lady from a house offered us some stew to keep us going, but then some twins from Sam and Jack's year came up to us and implied that we needed to go back to Matlock now and leave Bonsall to its stew, and Isy and Jo's Dating Agency just crumbled after that. All the commissions had been met with the same indifference, horror, or finger-pointing as the original "Jack March" song. I just don't think boys in Derbyshire in the early nineties were ready to have a love song tailor-made for them.

Writing a song definitely wasn't a good way to find a boyfriend, even though these days I know loads more chords and would surely rhyme *hippie* with *Mr. Whippy* and *Frenchie* with *Givenchy*. I didn't want one anyway, did I?

16

Isy never does find out how Romanians cook toast

My mum loves a project. If you say something like, "I wish rain didn't go on my glasses and make my vision blurred—oh, well," she'll come back the next day with a diagram for miniature windscreen wipers that attach to each lens rim. When I was growing up, she was, at various times, a nurse, a piano teacher, a school recorder teacher, a church organist, a dinner lady, and a bell ringer, but all the time she was doing those jobs, she was always beavering away at various inventions: working late into the night or dramatically leaping up from the table at Sunday lunch to scribble down an idea. Her career as a nocturnal inventor bore such fruits as the Hanger Softener, a sponge contraption that attaches to coat hangers to stop crease marks; the Pen Holder with a Pocket, a sponge tube for holding pens with a pocket on the side for erasers, which renders the pen unusable because the weight of the eraser drags it sideways; and, perhaps most impressively, the Lentil Piano, a felt beanbag stuffed with lentils past their sell-by date with the keys of a piano painted on it, for people who wanted to play the piano but didn't have one. The idea was that it would be good for practicing the more technical side, where the fingers have to go on certain keys. The problem was that whenever you "played" it, it sounded like someone pressing felt down onto lentils.

My dad was a scientist when I was growing up—something to do with lead. I've never really understood quite what, but he went to Romania once to test a lead furnace's safety standards, and all the workers were in the habit of frying their eggs directly on the furnace to eat for their lunches and he had to tell them not to do it, which pained him greatly. To me, frying eggs directly on the furnace sounded like just about the best thing in the world. I felt for him. I thought that having a dad who was a scientist wasn't that interesting. The most exciting thing that had happened in his job was that he'd had to ask someone not to fry an egg. I never realized it at the time, but my dad's iron work ethic and my mum's instinct to fight for a solution to a problem—even something as seemingly slight as a virtually indecipherable crease mark appearing in the shoulder of a shirt—were things they passed on to me. It's not so much "Grit your teeth and get on with it." It's more "See if those teeth can be replaced with a machine that can grind food into pulp and can also clean itself." There's a light at the end of the tunnel, and if it's the light of the oncoming train, maybe the driver'll stop and try out the new high-speed coffee cup holder.

"Do your arms ever get tired of holding books you're reading? Ever wish there was a kind of stand you could balance them on?" my mum asked as we ate dinner that night. I was texting Ben under the table.

"Mum going on about inventions as usual. Need to go to pub!" I sent it.

"I do, actually," I said to my mum. "What are you thinking?" She proudly got out her diagrams for the book stand.

THAT NIGHT, I lay awake listening to the clock chime every fifteen minutes (how had I ever managed to sleep as a child?) and looking at the brightly colored walls till I felt a bit sick. Ben still hadn't replied to my earlier text about the inventions, and of course I hadn't been to the pub—none of my mates lived here anymore. I'd contemplated donning my dad's flat cap and tweed coat and nudging in next to the guys perched along the bar at the Red Lion, the opposite of debutantes, their solid backs defiantly turned away from the action in the room. Not looking for salvation in their pints, like how I used to think of them during my years as a poet—just normal men who liked words with low numbers of syllables and drinks the color of foxes. They'd tell me not to worry about Ben texting back, that he was an Aussie git, that I had a whole lifetime to find someone. Then they'd nod imperceptibly at the barman, who'd get them their usual, and they'd say, "And one for Miss here," and I'd clink glasses with them, and all would be well for a bit.

One a.m. and he still hadn't replied. I picked up my phone and, without pausing to stop myself, texted, "Night x."

Two thirty a.m. and still nothing. I'd broken the rules by putting a kiss, and he still wasn't playing. Who was I kidding? You have to both want something other than what there is for there to be a game. There was no game. If one person starts playing Guess Who? and the other person's climbing Kilimanjaro, they're not going to be that invested in the game of Guess Who? At best, you're going to get, "Not Alfred! He looks well dodgy!" as they gaily clip their harness into place and disappear into the clouds, while you're left wondering why you always get bloody Anita. And of course when I say climbing Kilimanjaro, I mean shagging someone else. Probably.

At breakfast the next morning, Mum asked when I was going to visit Amy and Gavin and I started crying.

"I know what you need," she said immediately.

"No, you don't," I sniffled through my Shreddies. "I don't need a contraption to catch my tears and use them to fertilize vegetables."

"Come with me," she said, and she hauled me out of my seat, up the stairs, and to the most mysterious place in the house: The Computer Room. The Computer Room was the spare room, which had The Computer in it. With my parents' generation, you don't merely flip a laptop open and go online; there's a big mission involved. "We're going to The Computer Room. You never know what might happen. Let's take nuts and raisins in case we get stranded." We always have to make a cup of tea to take to The Computer Room—that's key—but then when we get there, there's lots of discussion about what to do with it—"Don't put it near the printer, please! It took Dad three hours to install that, and it still won't scan!"—so you end up holding the scalding hot cup between your thighs and they go redder and redder as Mum plays clips of Susan Boyle on YouTube and says, "I cry every time. *Every time.*" Using a mobile phone requires a similar amount of planning. A text is usually saved to drafts before being sent, and more often than not, it contains percentage signs or Chinese letters.

This morning, there was no tea or Susan Boyle business. Mum opened a dating website. I say "opened." She never just puts in the website address at the top, like everyone else does. She turns on the computer, triple clicks on the Internet icon, types in "www dot google dot com," presses ENTER twice, and then types the full website address into the search bar on Google. I used this lengthy period to protest profusely about the idea of going on a dating site.

"Darling," she said, "there's no pressure. We're just having a look." *We?* "It's try-before-you-buy." *Buy?*

"I'm OK, actually," I mumbled. "I'm not ready to meet The Actual One. I'm seeing an Australian."

"Are you?" She looked at me. "Where is he? There hasn't been an Australian in Matlock since 1997."

"No, Mum," I countered. "I mean, I'm sort of—you know— I'm not ready for a boyfriend. It's casual. I only split up with Sam—"

"Five months ago," she interrupted. Was it really that long ago? "And don't think I haven't noticed that this is your first visit since then, and you spend the whole time looking at your phone and sighing. I thought you hated people doing that at mealtimes."

"I *do* hate it!" I shouted. "Maybe I hate myself! Did you ever think of that?"

As I pushed back my chair, planning to scurry to my room and dig out Alanis Morissette's *Jagged Little Pill* on cassette, she got the site open, and I couldn't help but be staggered at the number of single men on it. Not just that, but they weren't all totally disgusting. I sat back down. It seemed wrong, almost voyeuristic, to be allowed to look at hundreds of men without putting my details online, but that was the offer the website was making. If there was someone you liked, you could pay to register. If there wasn't, no problem. Mum started to click on photos, ignoring my feeble protests. Despite myself, I began to enjoy looking through all these heartfelt profiles. I immediately realized that my mum's tastes and mine were very different (thank God). There was a half-Russian guy in a thick Irish sweater who I thought looked all right, but he was instantly dismissed by my mother because he was doing a master's: "He's avoiding reality. He'd make some kind of Russian soup, then just swan off."

It soon became clear that she thought I should be with a lawyer, GP, or judge, and I thought I should be with a potter, performer, or spy. I didn't even notice my phone bleep as we got sucked farther in, and as Mum got a pencil and paper and started to make a short list. There were a few we agreed on, and she noted down their usernames. Bizarrely, the fact that she was doing it in pencil rather than pen or, say, blood, made it seem like I could get out of it at any point. After about twenty minutes, as we both got particularly excited over a bloke who could ski backward, she made her proposal to me. The proposal was that she pay the fee for me to join, and I go on just one date with a man from the site *if* I hadn't found a boyfriend "by natural means" within a month.

"No way," I said. "I told you, I don't want a boyfriend."

"OK, then," she sighed patiently, as if talking to a five-year-old. "Let's have a cup of tea, and we can set up your profile, but we won't use it. Tell you what, we'll even do it in Microsoft Word." She pronounced *Microsoft Word* with self-conscious ease, like how a plucky Brit pronounces *jalapeño* while holidaying in Spain.

Tea is to blame for so much. Everything seems better and more solvable when you have that warm, golden liquid on your person. Even just holding a mug of tea makes me feel like I could possibly kill a buffalo if I really had to. Just as long as I could have this gorgeous cup of tea first. I sipped as Mum triple-clicked the Microsoft Word icon, and then I placed my mug dangerously near the printer, but she was oblivious. We decided on a photo—which took ages, because she wanted a combination of "wholesome and bright, but not domineering"—and, after laboriously pasting it into the document, we painstakingly started on the job of writing about me. She insisted on typing. First she put my religion as Christian, which I wanted her to change to atheist. We eventually compromised with agnostic. It was like when you're sharing dessert and you settle for crème brûlée or panna cotta. They can't cause offense. They're just *there*. Then she started on my tagline, as it were, to appear under my profile. "Fun-loving, sassy, and curvy," she gleefully typed out. No, no, no, a hundred times no. All of those are euphemisms. No one wants that on their gravestone. No one wants a euphemism of any kind on their gravestone.

In
Loving Memory Of
ARTHUR JONES
"A bit of a character!!"
1930 — 2001

The words *fun-loving, sassy,* and *curvy* have no meaning: they are obsolete currency, having been used in every Lonely Hearts column since 1981. She may as well have put "quirky, feisty, and unique." She paused pensively, resisting my shouts, and added: "Likes walks . . . maybe more." What did that mean?

"Everyone puts 'maybe more' in their profile!" she protested, trying to change each word into multicolored fonts as she spoke.

"Yeah," I said, "but they put 'maybe more' after sentences like 'looking for friendship' or 'looking for fun'—not 'likes walks.' What does 'likes walks . . . maybe more' mean? That while on the walk, we might leap hand in hand over cow dung or negotiate a tricky gate?"

"Oh, lighten up," she snapped. "It's quirky."

To be honest, I wasn't sure I'd do a much better job on my own. It's so hard to write a description of "you" when you're trying to sell yourself romantically to the right person. You're treading the thin line between typical British modesty and necessary confidence, which can so easily be misinterpreted as arrogance. Outdoorsy, fun, attractive, slim, medium build, intellectual, arty—each person had most likely thought about what to write as carefully as Mum and I were doing, yet all the adjectives started to lose their punch when we read them repeatedly. In the same way, the faces seemed to merge into one. Earnest men perched on hilltops in gray fleeces, grinning men in hopefully ironic—who's to know?—Hawaiian shirts at barbecues, contemplative men lying on generic beaches. After a while my head felt like it had after I'd played Pac-Man for four hours straight without any food or water and then couldn't listen to the Pac-Man music or eat Mini Babybels for months. Who cared what she wrote? We weren't going to put it online anyway, were we? I left her to it and dragged my fun-loving, sassy, curvy, quirky, feisty, unique ass to the kitchen to talk to my dad about why precisely it was a crime for the Romanians to fry eggs on a furnace and, more important, how the hell they cooked the toast.

As I walked downstairs, I saw that I'd had a text from Ben. It didn't address my text to him the night before about Mum's inventions, or my late-night one. Of course it didn't. It was a photo of him on his bike on Hampstead Heath, in a fleece, with the words "Happy daze." I gazed at it. This would be the photo *he'd* use on a dating site, for sure. He looked genuinely content, with laughter lines that were white in contrast with his tanned skin. And "Happy daze" would undoubtedly be his tagline. If I saw him on the site, I didn't think I'd click on his profile.

That evening over spaghetti Bolognese, Mum bombarded me with information about men's profiles at every opportunity she could. I feigned nonchalance while secretly putting them into Would/Wouldn't piles. After they'd gone to bed, I sneaked into The Computer Room and rewrote my profile, making it as human as possible, and then saved it in Word. The next morning she started up at me again like a woodpecker in the park, chipping away until the poor, exhausted tree finally gives up and falls down into the dog shit and empty beer cans. She was so excited, it was as if *she* were looking for a potential boyfriend, not me. As I emerged from the shower, she grabbed my arm, dragging me toward The Computer.

"I've found a brown-haired one who doesn't like cycling, either!" she gasped. "He likes acid jazz, though—is that OK?"

I sat down, drying my hair. She jubilantly gestured toward a photo of a serious-looking guy in glasses with a sporadic beard. Areas of the beard were long and wiry, next to arid patches of pasty skin. His mouth was wet and turned down at the corners, and he was really skinny; one of those types who can slip in and out of a room without anyone noticing. He looked like he'd use one of those free canvas bags you get from *The Guardian* as his main bag.

"I've drafted a message to him in Microsoft Word," Mum said.

"Go on, then," I said, smiling. "Show me."

She'd written: "Hi! My name is Isobel, but everyone calls me Isy! When I was little, I spelled it Issy, but now I spell it Isy. I live in London. Do you? What a busy place! I like your photo, although you look a bit tired! Was it at the end of a long day of lectures? I notice your a lecturer. Well done! Bye. Love Isy/Issy/Isobel/Call me what ya like!"

I looked at her eager little face.

"I'll tell you what," I said, "delete this message—and not because of the 'your.' But since this whole thing is obviously so important to you, why don't we do the deal? You can register me on the site, but that's it. If we reach the end of one month and I haven't found a boyfriend, you can message all the guys you want, and I'll go on a date with whichever one you choose. Even if they're on a bike."

Her eyes lit up, like in cartoons when an animal sees food or the opportunity to make a lot of dollars.

"Good," she said, "because I registered you last night." I scrambled to the computer. "With your rewritten profile," she added, her eyes twinkling. "I'm not as stupid as I look."

As I left to go back to London, I thought about what a massive favor she'd done me. I needed no greater kick up the arse than my mother potentially picking a boyfriend for me. I would undoubtedly win. In the meantime, she was welcome to her project of short-listing potential partners from the site, which I'm sure beat stuffing piano-shaped beanbags with gone-off lentils. Just.

17

Isy's A Level French fails her yet again

When I got back to London, the first thing I did was go out and get pissed with six other single women I knew. We all worked in the media in some capacity—about half of us were performers and half worked on the production side. I told them all about my mum's Internet challenge.

"Oh, we've got to do something about that!" said Michelle. "We can't have your mum pick a boyfriend for you!"

Michelle was going on a date the next day. She was going rock climbing somewhere on the outskirts of London with a guy she wasn't sure she fancied. We surmised that rock climbing is quite a good idea for an early date, as there will always be something to talk about. "Aren't rocks hard?" "Aren't rocks gray?" "Aren't rocks hard to grip?" and so on. I suggested that to test whether she fancied him or not, she should get him to complete tasks to do with the rocks, like climbing an advanced course, or leaping over some equipment that was lying by the side of the course, and then she should snog him if he passed the test.

Then we said, imagine if all seven of us went rock climbing with seven guys, and we got them to do tasks, and snogged them at the end if they did the tasks successfully. We got some more drinks. Then we said—OK, OK, then *I* said—imagine if we all went to a restaurant instead, and got seven guys to come, and didn't exactly get them to do tasks but got them to be themselves, and then we could see which ones we fancied at the end of the evening, and snog them. Ha! We got some more drinks. It got more detailed. We'd meet seven guys we didn't know in a restaurant, and each month—this was how the plan went—one of us girls would couple off with one. He'd become the boyfriend of the girl, and the next month there would be him plus six new guys, competing for the heart of one of the six remaining girls. The month after, there would be two couples and five new guys, and so on. Then, after seven months, we'd all have boyfriends. Someone's family owned a holiday cottage in Hampshire that all fourteen of us would then go to as a prize. We'd drink champagne or probably prosecco and all have sex with them. Our own, not each other's boyfriends—we weren't insane! It sounded like a wacky Scandinavian game show, or like the 1990s ITV show hosted by Chris Tarrant where a group of men competed for a date and were randomly pushed into a swimming pool to the jeers of a female audience when they didn't make the grade. We thought a swimming pool would be a bit much, so we settled for a curry house in the East End.

I'm pleased to report that the next morning, none of us woke up and put the whole thing down to too many bright blue cocktails. In fact, we were all even more excited about our plan. By that evening, Izzy, the most organized of the group, had drafted an advert for the current-affairs magazine *Private Eye* and also set up a Facebook page, to try to recruit a wide array of men. I waived my Facebook objections—after all, I've always said it's a good business tool, and we meant business. None of us wanted to reveal our true identities, so for the Facebook page, instead of a photo we used a silhouette of the women from *Charlie's Angels*. We called ourselves the Secret Seven, and the Facebook page said:

> We are a group of seven attractive female professionals who work in the media and live in London. We've decided to bypass online dating and have set up a series of dinner parties in various areas of London. If you join the group, we'll check out your profile and be in contact if we feel like you might be right for us and one of us might be right for you. This is in no way some kind of orgy, swingers' group, or food-based sex party, we're just trying to meet guys in a way that we think will allow a bit more time than speed dating and be relaxed and fun for everyone involved.

The *Private Eye* advert was the same, but asked them to apply. There was a lot of discussion around the word *attractive*, as we didn't want to come across as smug, yet we wanted it to be clear that we weren't all nauseating. *Dinner parties* is a bit of a euphemism, but the consensus was that we wanted to get "nice men" to reply. My objection was that we might get the kind of men who liked going to dinner parties, but I was overruled. The more we worked on the wording—all throwing e-mails to and fro with tiny adjustments, and transferring minuscule amounts of money into various accounts for the *Private Eye* advert—the more we got into it. How could this not succeed, with the number of hours we'd put in? There was something great about it being called the Secret Seven, like we were all in an Enid Blyton story. We set up the ad and Facebook page and confidently booked a fourteen-seat table at the aforementioned curry house for two weeks' time. That should give us ample opportunity to sift through the thousands of applications and choose the seven lucky winners we thought.

In the meantime, to hedge my bets, I decided to text Joe, the guy I'd met at the artists' party in Dalston.

"Hey Joe, fancy meeting up?" I texted. "From the Dalston party, it's Isy. No worries if you're busy."

I wasn't that fond of the last line, but I guess I wanted a nod to the fact that on the only occasion I'd met him, he'd spoken in rhyme. It's hard to find words that rhyme with *Isy*. *Dizzy* is too obvious. *Fizzy* is wrong. *Tizzy* and *whizzy* sound like cartoon characters, or drug dealers. And *jizzy*—it was too early for *jizzy*.

Even though I didn't really know Joe, I'd had a real laugh with him and had that horrible heart-not-quite-in-mouth-but-near-esophagus feeling as the minutes ticked by. I was with Sue in the kitchen, who was trying to distract me by playing a game where I guessed whether foods had gone off by tasting them, when my phone bleeped. I read the text out loud.

"You're alive! Friday at eight, meet at Farringdon station, 'tis a date. We can go to Dans le Noir, young Isy, drink red wine, and maybe get jizzy." Jesus Christ. He'd gone for *jizzy* in the first-ever text. Surely he meant *jiggy*, as in Will Smith's "Gettin' Jiggy wit It"? If he did, even that was pretty forward—but surely still better than the homemade cardigan—ed men my mum was lining up for me. And at least there wasn't a "your/you're" issue.

"You're and your" is quite a biggie for me, although I was much more hard-nosed about it in the past. It used to be that if you're a bloke and you get "you're" and "your" mixed up, and you use moisturizer: nil points. Your out on you're silky-smooth ear. Over the last few years, though, I've realized that (a) we don't have a Victorian education system anymore, so standards of grammar aren't quite as high, and (b) getting the two mixed up isn't, as I used to think, indicative of a deep-seated thickness or an inability to distinguish between two similar words—people can still be intelligent, or they might be dyslexic, and so on. However, I was pleased to see that he'd gotten it right. As for the moisturizer, unfortunately these days your boyfriend probably is going to use moisturizer, un-less you seek out a fifty-year-old farmer in Northumberland, but he's likely to have bigger problems, like a missing thumb, or an expectation that you'll cook all his meals in an iron pot over an open fire and eat silently while he shakes his head and mutters, "The farm int what it used t'be. Bloody Hargreaves's bull's getting ready for breedin' time again, and it's bigger 'n' better 'n ours. Best get used to eating gruel and nettles again. Let's 'ave me a suckle on yer teats afore I go and plough the wheat, Jizzy Isy." Actually, the farm option didn't sound that bad, but it was a long commute from London to Northumberland, and it was quite easy to get to Farringdon.

I glanced at his text again. Dans le Noir? I'd failed A Level French after writing a musical version of *The Stranger* by Camus that was all in the present tense and that I handed in on cassette tape—but even I could remember what Dans le Noir meant: "in the black." Did he mean he didn't owe any money, so he'd be paying? "Great," I texted back. "'Cos I'm Dans le Rouge!" No kisses yet. Just a trusty exclamation mark. "Haha!" came back. Ah—so he didn't have to speak in rhyme if it was an involuntary noise. All I had to do was perpetually make him laugh or cry. That shouldn't be too hard.

18

Isy sits on a stranger's lap

I placed my index finger in my empty wineglass and began to pour. It wasn't rocket science: when you feel the warm liquid touch the end of your finger, that means your glass is full enough. No use: it overflowed onto the lap of the man next to me for the second time.

"I'm so sorry," I gasped. "It's just hard 'cause I can't see anything."

"Don't worry," he breathed. "This is a common problem here. I'm wearing maroon."

REWIND A few hours. I'm slowly getting ready to go on my date with Joe, and Sue's perched on my bed.

"Have you ever noticed how much Al says the word *munch*?" she said, cutting off crescents of toenail and arranging them meticulously on my duvet. "He says it all the time. 'Shall we get something to munch?' 'I'll be there in a mo', I just need to munch my sandwich.' 'One cake'll be enough for both of us to munch on.'"

"Does he like *The Scream*?" I said, applying too much blusher. She cackled good-naturedly.

"Why does it piss me off so much?" she continued, returning to her toes.

"I dunno," I offered. "It's only a tiny thing, isn't it. Maybe it's a phase."

This was the first time I'd heard anything bad about Al. I was usually witness to a great camaraderie between Sue and him.

"Every time I hear it, I have an actual physical reaction," she lamented. "When he says it, I almost feel sorry for him."

She idly picked up my phone and started going through my texts.

"Oh wow, Dans le Noir!" she said. "I didn't know Joe was taking you there."

"Yeah, you did," I said. "I read that text out to you yesterday."

"You must have mispronounced it," she muttered, scanning the rest of it. "Dans le Noir is that restaurant where you eat in the dark. That must mean he really likes you. He wants to concentrate on just your voice, not think about your looks. Maybe he *is* The Actual One."

I started to get excited. And surely I didn't need to put too much effort in if we were going to be in the dark all night. He was going to see me for about eight minutes on the walk to the restaurant, and then about eight minutes on the walk back to the Tube. Assuming we spent a couple of hours eating, it only mattered 12 percent what I looked like. Result! I abandoned the search for an outfit and sat down next to Sue.

"Now," I said, peeling off my own bits of toenail to add to the pile that would inevitably end up on my carpet with all the others, "what's wrong with the word *munch*?"

I ARRIVED in Farringdon at about two minutes to eight. What a weird place Farringdon is. If you haven't been there, it's an area of East London that is a bit trendy but slightly off the beaten track—there's a really famous club there called Fabric, and quite a few bars, but there are also lovely old-man pubs and lots of businesses, and the streets are quite narrow and thin, like in the olden days. There are also two stations called Farringdon, one Overground and one Tube station, which stand directly opposite one another in a kind of face-off, like it's a competition. "You can use Oyster on *my* trains." "You can use them on mine, too, since June 2011." "We've got smoother escalators." "We've got fitter staff," etc., etc. As I came through the barriers of the Tube I realized that Joe hadn't specified which of the two we'd meet at, so when I got onto the street and tried to settle into The Position of Nonchalance, I had that horrible feeling where the person you're meeting for your date could be anywhere around you—you have to keep checking 360 degrees. I felt like Jason Bourne, minus the sixth sense for what was going to happen next. I wondered vaguely if Matt Damon had ever felt this. No—he must always meet women against the walls of ice-cream parlors or roller rinks.

I couldn't lean against the wall in case Joe was going to come from behind me, out of the Underground station, but then I couldn't face the Underground barriers themselves in case he emerged from the Overground, and also because that would look insane if he did walk toward me, like I was his mum waiting for him to come back from a music festival. "Did you have fun? Did you dance? Did you eat those apples I gave you?" Also, the two stations are on a busy road, so he might come on a bus, or even walk. He looked like the kind of guy who might walk places, just a fiver in his pocket, seeing what happened. Or ride a bike. The options were bloody endless.

I felt nerves pricking my skin. It didn't help that in line with not caring much how I looked, I was wearing a duffle coat, a midlength skirt, and black tights. I looked like an off-duty waitress who jazzed up her uniform with a sparkly brooch. My phone bleeped: Mum. "Good luck! Rang your house and Sue said you were on DATE! 录扼 麓 儋圓" The only reason we had a landline in our flat was so we could get the Internet. The only people who rang it were my mum and telesales robots. I put my phone back in my pocket and concentrated on looking cool. I decided that the best option was to turn around very slowly and methodically on the spot, like a ballerina in a music box whose batteries were running low. I started to hum to myself, too, as if waiting for him wasn't the most important thing I was doing. I feigned a look of introspection, as if I'd been tasked with solving the Hum.

As with all these things, it wasn't as dramatic as you're building it up to be—will he descend in a hot-air balloon? Has he had an accident on the way here and I'll be asked to identify the body?—and he just walked out of the Underground station a few meters to my left and caught my eye. He seemed to have had the same thoughts as me about not worrying too much about appearance—he was wearing baggy gray-green cords with blue Pumas and a black shirt. It kind of worked, and after all, *I* could hardly talk. I'm a sucker for nice sneakers. My favorite look is "nineties DJ on the wane." I like the kind of face that says, "I never get lost at a festival." Or "I look better the more I don't wash, but I also look good when I wash." Or "I can speak fluent German, but don't worry, I never will." Anyway, Joe wasn't far off. I couldn't believe that the last time I saw him, he'd been wearing suspenders and roller skates. It had definitely been ironic. He was normal. Happy days. Certainly not Happy Daze, dearest Ben.

As we walked to Dans le Noir, I told him about how I'd been wondering if he'd arrive on a bike.

"Fuck, no," he said. "I hate cycling."

"Me, too!" I gasped. This was a real boon. I told him about how when the gourmet food company had had an office in Fulham before it had gotten into trouble and moved to Battersea, I'd attempted to cycle to work. That was the only time I'd ever cycled in London. My mate had lent me a bike and told me to just relax. I'd done my cycling proficiency at school, hadn't I? I cast my mind back to primary school. A man had come in to give us lessons, who we all called Mr. Potato Head because he had had a bit of mashed potato near his right ear in the first lesson, and I'd spent most of the time drawing pictures of him rather than listening. I remember wobbling around the playground a few times, holding out my arm in an attempt to indicate, then getting distracted by David Swain's lovely head. I had my hair cut like David Swain's when I was ten because I was so in love with him. Don't do that. Ever. "Yeah, yeah, I've done cycling proficiency," I'd cackled in Fulham. How hard could riding a bike in London be? Loads of goons did it every day. Crack addicts did it.

I must have cycled for a total of ten minutes that day. I couldn't believe how hard it was. I couldn't drive, so I didn't know any of the rules of the road. In my desperation to stay on the street, I decided to just follow a car, copying everything it did so that I was supposedly abiding by the law, until I realized I couldn't cycle as fast as a car could drive. I couldn't believe I was expected to go around roundabouts. I couldn't believe that anyone could just get on a bike and do this. After ten minutes I cycled into a stationary police car, and then I just gave up. I got myself onto the sidewalk and wheeled my bike all the way to work. It felt so good to be on the sidewalk, with normal people. I suddenly appreciated everything around me—all the different grays at my feet, a nod from a friendly shopkeeper, even a dog pissing against a lamppost seemed beautiful and poetic. So in a way, cycling had made me really happy.

Joe laughed, then said, "It sounds like fun, in a round-about way. I've never even tried it, so what does that say?"

In my slight nervousness, I'd forgotten that he did the speaking-in-rhyme thing, because this was the first time he'd done it this evening—we'd had a perfectly normal conversation until now. Surely there was no way he was going to go in and out of rhyme all night. What did he do—formulate the thought, then swiftly decide whether to do it in rhyme or not? Maybe that last thing had been in rhyme by chance. But he couldn't claim he "didn't know he was doing it," like when people start each sentence with, "You know what?"—because it was the opposite: it actually took real effort and commitment. The whole night I was going to be braced for it, like when someone's cheated and they always might do it again. I decided to take the bull by the horns.

"Was that intentionally in rhyme?" I said, smiling broadly to show him I didn't mean it as too much of a criticism.

"Ooh, you got me!" he replied. "I just sometimes do it. I do a bit of different stuff. I'm sort of an actor, musician, artist, web developer, and poet."

Of course he was. He lived on a canal in Dalston.

"But my poetry isn't like that. I just sometimes speak in rhyme for the hell of it."

"Oh, OK!" I said. I didn't really know if I was any closer to knowing why, or how often he normally did it. I mean, was it OK if someone said, "I just sometimes kick people for the hell of it"? But wasn't this what I wanted, after all? I'd shunned the doctors and judges my mum had waved in front of my face, instead saying I only liked artistic men. I couldn't have my cake and eat it. Tonight, I wouldn't even be able to see if it *was* cake. And he didn't look like he had stanzas from *As You Like It* written on his bedroom wall, and he didn't roll down his spine then back up again midconversation, or say, like someone once did at drama school, "Guys! The verb is *to play!*" Apart from everything else, it wouldn't have rhymed.

When we got to Dans le Noir, I realized that it was quite upmarket and that most people hadn't followed the logic that if you can't be seen, it doesn't matter what you wear. Joe and I entered a lobby area, which was lit, and we were told to put all our belongings, including our phones, in a locker. I was glad about this. I hate people constantly looking at phones at dinner or in the pub. It's like they've got an extra limb attached to the end of their arm, or like there's another person present, another person who's made up of a trillion splinters of real people, but the most narcissistic elements of each of them. The prevailing ghost at the feast is the iPhone—always threatening to light up or squeal out during a beautifully timed anecdote about a dog at a wedding making off with a wheel of Brie in its mouth. At least when babies interrupt interesting conversation it's not their fault—unless they have a particular grievance with Brie—but when phones do it, our justified annoyance has nowhere to go. We can see the owner of the phone wrestling with the temptation to glance at the screen as we deliver the final line—"And then it was sick on a pashmina and some coats"—and their relief is palpable: they give a perfunctory chuckle as their finger simultaneously swipes the screen and they see that someone they used to work with has posted a picture of a view from a ferry.

Yet it's not enough, the view from the ferry. With social networking, as we consume the ticker tape of ferry views and mind-numbing updates about cupcakes, we simultaneously excrete it; we must keep eating more updates to avoid dehydration. Conversations are often now a tedious tug-of-war between real words and digital words, between spontaneity and neurotic introspection, with the etiquette blurry and confusing for all.

I proudly told Joe about my ticker tape/excretion meta-phor and he nodded sagely but didn't speak. Poor guy. He was probably trying not to speak in rhyme. Who was I to cast as-persions on him? If it was going to work out between us, I just had to accept it. I decided to ask him something that required a long answer, to give him the option to do it if he wanted to.

"Why do you think we're not allowed to take our phones in?" I asked.

After some deliberation, he said—in prose—that he thought it was because the restaurant didn't want us to "cheat" by using the light from them to look at the menus.

I wanted to make him feel like he could do it if he wanted to.

"I've got a question, so riddle me ree," I faltered. "How will we order if we can't see?"

Joe laughed. "Harder than it looks, isn't it?" he said, just a little coldly, before turning to the French guy at reception and asking what the protocol was. It turned out that we were to pick a type of meal off a laminated menu here and now, and some wine if we wanted it. The types were Meat, Vegetarian, and Surprise.

It was, in essence, a very expensive raffle. What could Surprise be? A punch in the face out of the darkness? A live spider in your wine? Jeremy Clarkson already sitting in your seat? Maybe they watched your behavior in the lobby and de-duced what your worst fear would be. As I wrote my name next to Surprise, my mind raced back over the brief conversation I'd had with Joe. We had to leave our credit cards at recep-tion, too, presumably in case, once inside, we escaped down a rubbish chute we found with the infrared monocles we'd smuggled in. What had I been talking about that they could surprise me with? I'd just harped on about mobile phones and ticker tape and excretion in a pretty self-important way. There were endless options for them there. Joe ticked Surprise, too, murmuring, "Live fast, die young!" He was right. *This* was life. Amy and Gav were probably sitting in their new living room watching *Monk* and drinking black tea because they'd run out of milk and the village shop closed at 5 p.m. Suckers. I was about to enter a dark, sweaty cave and consume overpriced wine and probably some bizarre sea creature, and possibly some other weird surprise substance.

After we'd handed our forms back to the bloke at reception, we looked around warily at the other diners who were assembled in the reception area. Everyone looked a bit nervous, and a few of them were making limp jokes about running off to the Indian restaurant down the road before it was too late. It was like the queue for the completely dark Black Hole roller coaster at Alton Towers—upon which I'd dumped my very first boyfriend so I didn't have to see his reaction—except this roller coaster was going to take approximately two hours and, as far as I knew, we weren't going to get a photo of ourselves afterward, mouths open somewhere between trepidation and horror, eyes midblink.

Suddenly a waitress popped out from behind a red velvet curtain that I realized must lead into the restaurant.

"Hi everyone!" she said. "I'm Sarah! I'm going to take this group of you through now. Get into a line and hold on to the person's shoulder in front of you, and I'll lead you into the restaurant and to your seats."

She read out our names and told us to get in line in that order. I'd been told that all the waiters and waitresses were blind, and I was so impressed with how well Sarah knew the layout of the restaurant. Mostly because, rather than its being a few small tables scattered around behind drapes as I'd imagined, people were huddled in close together. Our line traipsed through the restaurant, squirming and giggling. It sure was pitch-black. You couldn't see a single thing. I was at the back of the line and felt very vulnerable, like someone was going to slap my bum or put a custard pie down my back.

When we eventually got to our seats—which was heralded by her saying our names and telling us to sit—I actually sat directly onto a man's lap. I couldn't believe how close together the seats were. Thankfully, it wasn't Jeremy Clarkson; it was a man called Dave, and his girlfriend, Lisa, was opposite. They were to be a lifeline for Joe and me, as they'd been to Dans le Noir, or Le Noir as they called it, multiple times: they were old pros. They gave us lots of tips: Put your finger in your wineglass to feel how much you're pouring in. Don't even bother trying to use a knife and fork—eat with your hands. No heavy petting. Dave laughed when he said that one and swiftly added, "Not really, this is a great place for it." His hand brushed my knee. Fuck. Were they swingers? Was this the Surprise? I had no idea what he looked like. How could I make a decision about a foursome with this handicap?

Luckily our starters arrived, and, as we all know, if anything's going to put the kibosh on group sex, it's a prawn cocktail. At least that's what we thought it was, but we couldn't be sure. Everything on our plates felt and tasted warm, moist, vaguely lumpy, and not unpleasant. Since we'd picked Surprise, it could be anything in the world.

When Sarah brought our mains, I timidly asked what mine was.

"*I* don't know!" she answered, placing our plates carefully down in front of us on the tiny table. "I'm blind!"

"Yes!" I stuttered, adding, in the most middle-class way possible, "It's incredible!"

She laughed, obviously used to bumbling idiots like me. "The chefs don't tell us what the dishes are," she said, "or everyone'd ask. Enjoy the surprise."

19

Isy has nothing to say to John Lennon

The thing about the FTSE Index is, no one really gets it, even though they pretend to," Dave bellowed from the neighboring table.

"Yeah!" chuckled Lisa. "It's like the music of Prince—it's always kind of evolving, so there's no point in really trying to get a grasp on it. You've just got to let it wash over you."

"AH!" I shouted back, which sounded aggressive, since those little interjections aren't really designed to be shouted. The four of us didn't have much choice but to all chat, because when you can't see people, there's just noise from all directions hitting you, so you focus equally on each sound. Since no one could see anything at all, there were regular cries from diners to their waiters and waitresses, such as, "Sarah! Sarah! Are you there? I need the toilet, Sarah!"

Joe shouted from opposite me, "I guess the moment you

think you understand the FTSE Index, it goes and changes its name to a symbol!"

Silence from Dave and Lisa's side.

"Like Prince!" I added. I had no idea what they were thinking. I wanted to smile at Joe, but of course, we couldn't see each other. We were in one of the strangest restaurants I'd ever been to, in the pitch-dark. I kicked him gently under the table, then thought he might think I was trying to initiate a game of footsie, which I wasn't, but I wasn't completely opposed to it, either. He kicked me back once. I was about to make a joke on the similarity in pronunciation of FTSE and footsie when our desserts arrived, which were the nicest thing.

I was probably halfway through the date and I'd found out as much about Dave and Lisa as I had about Joe—who lived on a boat, I suddenly remembered. What if we went back and I got seasick? Could you get seasick on a canal? Canal sick? Although the novelty of Dans le Noir had blunted the edges of the first-date nerves, it had also diluted the finding-out-about-each-other element. Joe was naturally relaxed and seemed fine with eating in the dark, whereas I was petrified that I'd emerge back into the light of the lobby with a face covered in chicken or octopus or whatever the hell it was we were eating. And how could I tell if Joe was right for me when I couldn't see any of his expressions? It wasn't good to go on a date with the pressure of finding The Actual One, but the bet with Mum had added some urgency to matters.

Dave and Lisa worked in stocks and shares and had been married for six years, they told us as they shoveled mush into their mouths with their hands, like ravenous urchins in expensive suits. Or so I assumed. When the four of us tentatively emerged onto the street, having decided to go for a drink at the pub next door, I was astonished to see that Dave had bum-length very straight mousy brown hair, and a kind of druid's outfit on—a long purple-and-black robe. Lisa looked more conventional in a flowery dress, but green eyeliner hinted at the alternative woman beneath.

I didn't know too much about druids. My only experience with druids was that when I was a teenager, I got heavily into Ouija boards and started to do them all the time. My mum had taught me how to do it one day, as there were kids in an American book I had who were doing a Ouija board and I didn't know what that was. I used to do them very frequently when I got in from school, alone, writing out all the letters and numbers on a piece of printer paper and saying to a two-pence coin, "Spirit of the coin, I believe in you," until it started moving. And whether you believe in these things or not, it mostly worked. I think you tap into some energy within yourself, to be honest, but on the occasions I did them with other people it was always incredibly clear if someone was moving it. There's a real buzz when it moves "on its own."

I spoke to so many people over the years: soldiers, people who'd died of the plague, people from Norway. You just keep saying, "If anyone's there, please say yes"—a bit like when you're searching for your waiter or waitress in Dans le Noir—until it does, and then you ask it to spell out its name; it's a real grab bag. Or unlucky: the board once said it was my ghost from the future—although it spelled my name *Izzy* and I did give it a head start by immediately gulping, "Are you my ghost from the future, after I've died?" after which it was pretty easy for it to answer yes. The only question I could think to ask it was how many times I would have sex in my life. It said 40,385 times—I know because I wrote it down and put it in a shoebox with a picture of Hunter from *Gladiators* and a lock of David Swain's hair. I asked the ghost if that counted "in and out," which someone from school had already done at the rubbish dump, but it said no. Then we got a bit bored, so we asked it to go and fetch John Lennon. My ghost from the future was a bit put out, in my opinion, as it took a long time to say yes, and even longer to fetch John. When John finally arrived, we were so starstruck we didn't know what to ask him, so we were just like, "I love your music! Are you OK up there? You're great!" Looking back, it could have been any John.

The druid experience came out of the Ouija board one. When I got to about sixteen, I decided to stop doing Ouija boards because I met a couple of people in Glastonbury who said it wasn't a good idea. Not at Glastonbury Festival but in Glastonbury itself, which is teeming with people who seemingly went there for the festival, lost their ruby slippers, and never made it back home: a kaleidoscopic Bermuda Triangle. Tourists seeking out local ruins weave their way through tie-dyed leggings and bongos and fifty-year-old women dressed as fairies with face paint cracking around their eyes. The hippie couple was in a café, and I got talking to them about doing the Ouija boards regularly. The guy kept saying, "For sure, for sure." He must have said it about two hundred times in ten minutes—it was like breathing for him. It was a pity he didn't work for Sure deodorant, as, no matter how many drugs he took, he would always have been able to find his way to work, like when kids have their names and addresses written in their coat lining. Anyway, they said I should stop doing Ouija boards, as I was carrying around all the debris of the spirits I'd talked to, like a smelly old cloak, and I should get exorcised. Their mate did exorcisms and they could probably get me 10 percent off. At this point, their mate—it was unclear if this was the mate who did the exorcisms—came into the café with a mushroom box on his head, danced around all the tables, threw it into the fire, and then took a scone from the counter and paid with three crystals.

I decided I'd be OK without the exorcism but that I probably should stop doing Ouija boards. I let it be known that I was no longer the person who would "kick off" a Ouija board at a party—people would just have to do it on their own. It wasn't my fault I had the Midas touch. Instead, I decided to try to have an out-of-body experience. I had a magazine that had an article about out-of-body experiences, and there was a really simple-looking step-by-step guide to having one, like a cake recipe. I remember it as something like:

1. Lie flat on your back.
2. Make your head face the north.
3. Close your eyes.
4. Imagine yourself floating slowly out of your body.
5. Look down at your body!
6. Wow!
7. Imagine yourself floating back down into your body.
8. Now do it.
9. Open your eyes.
10. Have a nice cup of tea.
11. Go on, have a biscuit.
12. Naughty.

So one night I got onto my bed and lay with my head to the north—I'd had to ask my dad where the north was—and followed the rest of the instructions. For ages it didn't work, but after some patience my body twitched a bit and I felt like I was trying to rise out of it, and then I opened my eyes and thought I saw what looked like a druid at the end of my bed. I had to sleep in my parents' room, between them, for the next few nights. After that I decided to abandon the occult altogether. The druid business, along with my ghost from the future blatantly sending someone to "fill in" for John Lennon, didn't quite line up with my idea of what being "spiritual" should entail.

By this point, we were sitting in the pub next door to Dans le Noir.

"You did the right thing," said Dave, solemnly. "You've got to know what you're doing with that shit."

I wondered if he was a real druid—whether he knew what *he* was doing, or whether he just liked dressing up as one, like the women on the hen night in Plymouth who were dressed as nurses, all of them praying that there's no real emergency, that no one gets punched in the nightclub, because all they can do is pour Jägerbombs on the wound and clamp the person's head on their sticky breasts, softly singing "Come On Eileen." I supposed there was no law against druids or white witches working in finance—I just couldn't imagine Lisa and Dave in a meeting room, drinking coffee from polystyrene cups and pointing to whiteboards. Dave's hair was so long, the only way he would have been able to conceal it would be to put it in a ponytail but then feed it down under his shirt and into his underpants, his split ends playfully caressing his buttocks as he explained the latest money figures.

In the loo, I looked at my phone. There were two texts. The first was from Mum. "How is date??! If unsuccessful got good one lined up. Interior designer and lives near you! &%$$$." The second was from Izzy. "No replies to Secret Seven yet. Maybe we should put real photos on?" I didn't want to do that. Back at the table, I asked Dave and Lisa how they met.

"We met online," they said. "In a gaming forum."

Then they snogged, in a way that was like a punctuation mark, sealing the fact. I thought it was time Joe and I made a move. Why do I always order pints?

At the station, Joe and I said bye, then got on the same train, like in a sitcom. We talked about Dave and Lisa, plunging ourselves into the topic so we didn't have to talk about each other or whether we'd go on another date (we wouldn't). It wasn't just that there was no real spark between me and Joe, but I also suddenly wanted someone sensible—an engineer, a train driver. Not even Ben, who texted me and asked if I wanted to come over. I wanted Sue, tinned peaches, cream, and to start thinking about what I was going to wear to Secret Seven.

20

Isy discovers that French women probably do try dresses on first

The Secret Seven was having a crisis meeting. We'd still had no interest on the Facebook page. There was a smattering of "likes," but they were mostly from our mates in the know, trying to show their support, or amusement, toward our scheme. There had been sparse replies to the *Private Eye* advert. Of the few that we got, the men were either over fifty or blatant pervs—none suitable. When we sent kindly worded rejection messages to them, one of them replied, calling us all bitches. IN CAPITALS. We didn't know what to do, and then someone suggested the inevitable. That we might get more interest if the meal was in costume.

I hate dressing in costumes, perhaps because I'm an actor. My dislike of it stems from drama school, where there were so many costume parties that most of us had a basic one that we customized each week. I think costumes are fine if you're an accountant who spends lonely hours rehearsing a Yoda voice in front of the mirror for its one outing, but we were drama students. We spent every day barking like dogs and rolling around like babies, and hours, literally hours, being a lizard that turned into a character with the qualities of a lizard and then back into a lizard. We did not need to dress up on the weekend. It was a busman's holiday, and what's more, the bus was full of men in Lycra singing songs from *Les Misérables*.

One week in the second year, I attended my last-ever costume party. It was at Richard Hardwick's house, and the theme was characters from films. I went as Mia from *Pulp Fiction*, Uma Thurman's part, because I had a black bobbed wig left over from a show. I duly bought a tight black backless dress without trying it on, as I imagine French women do, got it home, put it on, and realized that unless you were an A cup, it didn't work. The weight of my boobs dragged the material at the front downward and outward, like they were cats trying to escape from under a rug. I didn't have any time or money to choose a different outfit. Panicking, I suddenly remembered something. On the TV show *This Morning* a few weeks earlier, a lady had been giving tips on how to wear different dresses, and she'd said that if your back's on show and you don't have a backless bra, you can put Band-Aids on your nipples, then stretch a few pieces of masking tape across the old chaps. That would keep them in place, and no one would know.

Time was ticking, and I had to work fast. I looked in the kitchen drawer in my student house and found batteries, un-paid bills, an old tea towel, a rubber thimble (why?), a chewed pen top, and some package tape. My mind was racing. Package tape. Package tape. What would the lady on the telly say about that? Surely masking tape was the same as package tape. Package tape was just brown as opposed to white, and wider—which would surely hold them in place even more efficiently. Yes, I would use the package tape and then I'd write to the lady on Monday and tell her I'd found something even better. I was sure we wouldn't have any Band-Aids, so I skipped the nipple bit—I quickly taped about four long strips of package tape over my chest, pressing down until I looked like I was playing a boy in Shakespeare, had another swig of vodka, and trotted off.

The party was like always—people packed into every crevice of the house, someone trying to climb into the washing machine, lots of glitter, a first-year crying and singing a song from *Rent* at the same time—and I was about to go home when I saw a third-year called Simon with slicked-back hair, a cashmere V-neck with no shirt underneath, and quite wide-legged jeans with cowboy boots. This sounds like a costume but was actually his everyday "look"—I knew because I'd fancied him for ages, in that way you fancy people in the year above you because they're in the year above you and for no other reason. Tonight, fueled by vodka and package tape (thank you, WHSmith!), I started up a conversation, and we ended up stumbling back to his.

As soon as we entered his room, he went to the TV at the end of his bed and put News24 on. I wondered why. It was four a.m. Was he waiting for the results of some foreign election, or was he so into current affairs that he had to have it on in the background all the time? It turned out to be the latter. Rather than abandon ship, I forced myself to see it as adding a kind of dangerous element, like we were doing this *right under the reporter's nose* and he had to carry on reading the news like nothing was wrong.

Then Simon uttered something I'll never forget. Like my first plane journey and the day I found a white hair in my eyebrow growing horizontally, it's etched into my brain for eternity. He kissed me, took hold of my chin, looked into my eyes, and said, "And how's Mrs. Mimsy?"

I racked my drink-befuddled brain. Who was Mrs. Mimsy? Someone at the party? He cast his eyes down to my crotch, then back up. A giggle bubbled in my throat as I realized what he meant.

"Oh, she's fine!" I grinned. "Never been better."

I thought that might seem a bit full-on, so I added, "She's bearing up." *Bearing up?* That made it sound like she was recovering from flu. Or herpes. He obviously didn't mind, as he kissed me again. "Good," he whispered.

At this point he pressed his body to mine, and there was a small but insistent crinkling sound. With horror, I recalled the package tape. Could I just keep him away from . . . what were they? Mrs. Mimsy's wayward twins? The fumbling continued, with me awkwardly rounding my back away from him, and again there was the unsettling sound from beneath my dress.

"Hang on, Simon, I'm just going to the loo," I said.

I considered leaving, but I hate giving up. The door locked, I surveyed the situation in the mirror. The strips of tape weren't separate anymore—there was just one fat wodge of package tape leading to each armpit, where the tape became scrunched into a ball with little peaks of skin pinched in it. When I counted to three like my mum used to and ripped the whole sorry thing off, I realized why the lady had said to put plasters over the nipples. Normally anemic looking, they were now an angry crimson. The skin was either a furious red where it had been trapped or stark white where it had been deprived of blood, and the whole area was covered in unnerving peaks and troughs. I went back into Simon's room, ready to come clean, and he'd fallen asleep in front of News24. So it did have its benefits after all. I vowed after that never to go to a costume gathering of any kind again.

When they heard my package tape story, the other members of the Secret Seven started to *insist* that we do it in costume.

"No way," I said. "Also, it doesn't solve the fact that we've got no guys."

Michelle interrupted with an idea. Why didn't we contact a dating site of some kind? They'd have loads of single guys. I thought of the men who Mum and I had viewed on the site. How would we even word the message? Mum knew about Secret Seven and, of course, thought it was a fantastic idea. I admired her sporting spirit, her not caring whether she or I "won," but I didn't feel equally generous minded about the prospect of her finding me a life partner.

21

Isy finds out how a South African man got his shirt so white

Our restaurant booking only days away, I was starting to write off the idea of the Secret Seven altogether when, true to her promise, Michelle found a guy who ran a dating page on Facebook who said he could help. A few of us met up with him at the Soho Theatre that night, to see if he could possibly ferret out seven normal men for us in the nick of time. I still had my doubts. Alex was a tall South African man who knew a lot about Internet dating—which I suppose this was a form of, much as we hastened to deny it—and was full of advice for us.

"You should have put more details about yourselves," he told us. "The word *attractive* is too vague. You should have put photos of yourselves."

"We didn't want anyone to know it was us, though," I said. "What could we have done, pixelated our faces?"

"Sure," he replied, not breaking a smile.

"Erm," Michelle said. "That might make us look like witnesses to a crime."

"A body's a body," Alex replied drily, but with a twinkle. "A body's a body."

At the end of the night, we were much wiser as to how to recruit men for the following month, but on the same level of panic about how to find seven eligible men in the next few days.

"Don't worry," Alex smiled. "I'll find you seven men. I'm single, so I'll be one of them, so that's"—he paused—"six."

I vowed not to sit next to him. If he couldn't even subtract one from seven, what hope did he have on the "your/you're" front? It was very kind of him, though. He would find men from his Facebook dating page and, failing that, address book, and they would all be there on Friday.

"Just wear your glad rags, girls," he winked as we parted, "and leave the rest to Alex."

I'm never sure about people who refer to themselves in the third person, except for boxers, and I wasn't sure that boxers wore loafers with socks.

On my way to the restaurant on Friday night, hair diffused, legs reluctantly bald, and wondering what lay ahead, I thought about when my sister had been speed dating a couple of weeks before. A guy had sat down opposite her, the clock had started, and he'd said, "If you were any character from *Sex and the City*—" and my sister—who can be very honest—had just gone, "No." And then they sat in silence for the remaining fifty-four seconds. I hoped none of them would be like that tonight. I was terribly nervous. It's strange how you can care so much about what a group of potentially unimportant strangers thinks of you. The idea of having a booger hanging out of my nose or a bit of eyeliner on my cheek was too much for my brain to handle. I suppose it's because you've put yourself on the line—you've said, "I want to find a partner." You're asking people to make a yes/no decision about you. At least my sister's response to the *Sex and the City* line had been quick and easy to read. I didn't want any blurred lines.

I got to the restaurant, slightly late, and as promised, there were seven guys sitting round the table. They looked as nervous as I did. Izzy had seated everyone girl/boy/girl/boy, and thankfully told me where to sit. Alex was beaming at the head of the table, and the other guys were taking quick sips from drinks and making staccato conversation with the girls next to them. All the men, bar one, looked virtually the same. They were all South African, all tanned, all in white shirts with three or four buttons undone, all worked in IT, and all had meaningful-looking carvings on leather strings hanging around their necks. The one who didn't look like them was the only one of the lot who didn't already know Alex—someone who had applied to his dating page. He was an actor from Blackpool, he wasn't bad-looking, he didn't have an ethnic symbol around his neck: ergo, he was my most reliable option. I'd said I wasn't going to go for anyone arty, but beggars can't be choosers.

After we'd ordered our food, the actor said he was going to go for a smoke, so I, annoying social smoker that I then was, trooped up the stairs with him. We were the only two. You see that in smokers, that shared relief when they realize there's another of them in their midst. "Oh, they smoke, too!" It knits you together temporarily—the ritual of getting them out, digging around for a light, talking about the other one's brand choice. For a moment it's like you're back at school. As we smoked, I deduced that he was a nice guy but that I didn't fancy him and he didn't fancy me. Mission accomplished. All that meant was that I could now relax and get drunk, as I wouldn't be one half of the couple who found each other tonight. For, of course, there would be one each month. That was how we'd planned it, so that was how it was going to work.

The actor and I got back downstairs. He sat back in his seat next to Zoe and I went to my place opposite. Zoe looked at him as he sat down and I thought I could tell that she fancied him, so I mouthed at her, "You can have him."

"What?" she mouthed back.

I mouthed again, overenunciating, "You can have him."

The actor clocked me this time. He mouthed, "Did you just say, 'You can have him'?"

I mouthed back, with a puzzled expression, "Did you just say, 'Did you just say, "You can have him"?'" He gave a watery smile, so I did, too, then I concentrated intently on the condiment in front of me, cheeks beetroot.

Halfway through the meal, a few of us rammed ourselves into the toilets to discuss how it was going. It quickly materialized that none of us had catered to the possibility that more than one girl would fancy the same guy. Two girls fancied one of the South African guys, and each of them gallantly agreed to let the other one have him. Then we decided to give him the option to choose.

Back in the room, the guys obediently moved along two places. This would happen every half hour, when either Alex or Izzy would stand up, clap their hands together, and say, "Come on, move along, guys!" I looked at the new guy on my left, suddenly feeling that fatigue you get at a wedding when you first sit down. My mind contained no topics whatsoever. Not even "Do you like music?" or "What's your name?" I settled for a "Hm!" and a raise of eyebrows as I started to spoon Madras curry onto my plate. The kind of all-encompassing "Hm!" that can mean anything—anything from "This is pretty cool, huh?" to "It's too crowded in here."

"Yeah," he replied, dissecting a poppadom.

I concentrated on spooning Madras onto my plate. I was glad I'd ordered Madras now. I adore hot food but at the time of ordering hadn't known whether to go superhot because of the actor-shaped window of opportunity that might turn into a shed of sex later in the evening, but I had gambled on it anyway, concluding that if he was going to be my husband he was going to see worse than me experiencing the aftermath of Madras during rapturous passion. Now I was glad I'd gambled. I didn't fancy any of them, so I could eat all the chili peppers I wanted! Hang on, nothing was at stake, so none of my actions mattered, did they? I was like a character in an existentialist novel! I didn't have to tentatively say "hm" to people: I could do anything! I left the first guy to his poppadom.

"How *did* you get your shirt so white?" I gabbled to the guy on my right. I was on fire! Mentally, and physically!

It turned out that the actor didn't fancy any of us. What

the hell?! This certainly wouldn't happen in the Scandinavian game show. There would be another Secret Seven in a month, but, because of the bet with Mum, that was too late for me. By then, the way things were going, I'd be in the arms of an accountant from Swindon who lists "shooting the breeze" as one of his hobbies.

22

Isy has cause to remember how to do a Girl Scout reef knot

I hope you don't mind," my mum's gleeful voice tinkled on the answering machine. "But I've been logging in and messaging a few potentials. Only two days to go now! Don't worry, I've been vague and said you sometimes work on an oil rig, so they won't be hurt if you don't end up going on a date with them."

There's no greater impetus to action than your mother writing to men she's handpicked from the Internet, pretending to be you. If I didn't find a boyfriend in the next forty-eight hours, I was done for.

I texted her. "Did you really put an oil rig? How am I going to explain that if I end up meeting them?"

"Haven't you gigged on an oil rig?" she replied. Of course I bloody hadn't. "If not, say you have!"

For once, there was an absence of Chinese letters and

dollar signs. Maybe all this contact with technology was sharpening her skills, at last. One good thing could come from this.

That night, drinking in the last-chance saloon, I went to a party at Caroline and Bobby's in Dalston. I took Sue and Al along. There were always legendary parties at Caroline and Bobby's. Not like the one in the artists' commune, just house parties like there were in the nineties. A recent one had culminated in Bobby—a builder—and his cousin Joel picking up an actual staircase and moving it a few meters, just to see if they could. On the bus on the way there, Al used the word *munch* twice.

"I feel like having something to munch," he murmured, gazing out the window at a kebab shop. And about twenty minutes later: "Will there be something to munch at the party?" The second time, Sue looked at me and widened her eyes as if to say, *I told you!*

"There will definitely be something to munch at the party, Al," I assured him. "You can munch to your heart's content."

He looked delighted at this. I had to leave Sue to sort this one out herself. I was on a mission tonight. The bus sailed toward Caroline and Bobby's, past the road where the artists' party had been. I remembered my and Joe's date at Dans le Noir. I hoped he was happy in his boat. Now the idea of us as a couple seemed utterly senseless.

The party was as good as ever, and before long, everyone was dishing out dares, having a break-dancing contest, and downing shots of vodka and milk because Joel had been sent out for mixers and hadn't arrived back yet. Al was happy with the snacks. Sue surveyed the room and decided that all the men were too skinny to be a potential mate for me. I surveyed the room and decided that there was only one guy who was half—all right—Caroline and Bobby's neighbor who I'd met a few times, Will. Will was a lawyer and often wore a black or purple coat with wide sleeves, a bit like a cloak. I could never decipher whether this was for work or not—I don't know much about the world of law—and if not, whether it was ironic or not. Irony is the excuse for everything now. "Oh, I'm not really smoking a pipe—it's ironic!" Is it? You know actual smoke's going into your actual lungs, or are they ironic, too?

Will had meringue-y yellow hair like a chick's fur, and the eyes of Boris Becker—the balls and lashes so pale, it was as if they needed a few more minutes before they were done. They gave him a certain vulnerability as he swished his cloak around and muttered about subpoenas. Like lots of people who work in law, the health service, or the police, he reveled in informing people that TV shows depicting his line of work weren't accurate. "*The Wire*'s fun, but it never happens like that. People sometimes go to the toilet. And there are really long pauses." I'd gotten into one of those conversations with him tonight. We'd been there for a few hours now, and the party was in full swing. Swaying slightly and sipping my vodka and milk, I tried to get him to tell me about his actual latest case in return for me telling him what I'd eaten when I did jury service, but he seemed to think this wasn't a fair swap.

My phone bleeped—Mum, of course. "What do you

think? Really nice civil servant, in five bands, used to have neck tattoo but says now completely lasered off." He must have impressed her for her to brush that fact aside. Time was of the essence. I chatted harder to Will. Another bleep. "Just told me it was more on shoulder than neck anyway, and at back. Says you can still see it in certain lights but have to look hard. It was only of Daffy Duck. Don't know why he bothered to laser off!! Does he sound OK?"

I had to make a plan, fast. I was good at thinking outside the box in order to try to make things happen romantically. When I was in my first year of drama school, I went out with a guy from my year: a tall guy called Jim. I say "went out": our relationship mostly entailed the two of us hunched in his living room, eating Weetabix with water because we couldn't afford milk, me gazing at all his Cher albums and repeating to myself that Jim definitely wasn't gay and of course he was just bi. It was Guildford in the late nineties! Nobody drank instant coffee anymore, people had finally thrown away their Hypercolor T-shirts, and everyone was bi, right? He could have his Jake Gyllenhaal and eat it, too. I just needed to do something to convince him to like girls *some* of the time. That would be good enough for me.

One day, I had a brain wave. Jim was due to come round in half an hour, but I would go and meet him halfway as a surprise. I ripped off my tracksuit bottoms, dressing gown, and everything underneath, and wriggled into my sexiest outfit: an overlarge fake fur coat, cadaver fresh from a charity shop, that was a disturbing mouse-dropping-gray color. It reached my midthighs and ended with the fur becoming dark and crusty because the bottom of it had been repeatedly marinated in dirt, puddles, and lager. On my feet I wore sneakers, because I hate wearing heels—even though I've worked out that they make me look 8 percent better—and also, I had to walk a good twenty minutes along the multilane road in order to intercept him. Even though I didn't look as sexy as I had in my head, it was the thought that counted. He wouldn't be able to believe his luck, and then we'd have sex in a tunnel or graveyard. It wasn't a warm night. I considered traveling on my classmate's skateboard, which he'd left at my house; then I could get there really quickly. I even tried a couple of circuits of our front yard but decided that now probably wouldn't be the best time to learn.

A spring in my step—well, they *were* foam soled—and adrenaline in my veins, I set off on foot. The first thing to happen that I hadn't legislated for was that cars immediately started to beep and wave at me. *Why are you beeping?* I thought. Then I realized. I looked like a prostitute—albeit a prostitute with dreams of becoming an aerobics teacher. In hindsight, I'm not sure the cars thought I was a prozzy. I'm no expert on the matter, but I don't think the traditional way to hail a prostitute is to beep and wave, like you're saying bye to your neighbors before you set off for a weekend break in Rhyl.

I kept looking for Jim across the ribbons of traffic, in case he was on the other side of the road, but I'd definitely not passed him, and I eventually reached the end of his road. Before mobile phones, there were fewer options. There was less lateness, no tormented discussions about texts. Back in the day, you had to haul your sorry mothball-covered, Ariel-white ass into a piss-stained phone booth and ring your boyfriend's landline, inhaling the potent fumes of Wrigley's and onions from the indented dots of the receiver. It was like a lovely little play:

JIM: Yup, hello?

ISY (*husky*): Hi, Jim, it's Isy.

JIM: Why are you talking so low?

ISY (*normal*): Hi, Jim, it's Isy. What you doing?

JIM: Why? Messing about with floppy disks. Are you in a phone booth?

ISY: When are you leaving?

JIM: In a bit.

ISY: How big a bit?

JIM: An indeterminable bit.

ISY (*twists curly receiver wire into mouth, remembers where she is, spits it out*): Hmmm. Ughmmmm.

JIM: See you in a bit.

ISY: Yup. I've got a surprise for you!

JIM: Did you buy milk?

ISY: Better than that.

JIM: A poodle!

ISY: No.

JIM: Bye.

ISY: Bye.

Time was of the essence. I was older and wiser now. I didn't go for gay guys, I wore heels slightly more, and I'd thrown the manky fur coat away. What could I do to snare Will the Lawyer?

Will had a cat named Bogey, after Humphrey Bogart. Bogey was black and white, like a cat in a children's story, and basically lived at Caroline and Bobby's because Will worked a lot. They even bought food for him. Bogey was like most cats—sweet, fickle, and deliciously selfish. I didn't mind Bogey and he didn't mind me. So when, unseen by Will, I carried him up to Caroline and Bobby's room, Bogey didn't protest. Bogey did protest when I placed him firmly on the disheveled bed and slammed the door on him before he could get out, but that didn't matter. I could hear him starting to meow as I pelted downstairs and grabbed Will from where he was attempting to do the robot to Morcheeba in the living room.

"Hey, Will," I gasped, "I think Bogey's trapped in Caz and Bobby's bedroom!"

"Trapped?" he said, blinking his milky lashes. "What do you mean?"

I hadn't thought this through. What *did* I mean? "I think you should come and see for yourself," I said, lightly taking his hand.

"Is he OK?" Will gasped as we mounted the stairs. He seemed to have sobered up completely with worry, poor guy.

"Yes, yes, he's fine," I said, turning toward the bedroom door, regretting my use of the word *trapped*. Incessant meows of fury were coming from behind the door, coupled with scratches and clunks as Bogey hurled himself against the inside of the door. I opened it with trepidation, expecting him to launch himself at my head, claws unfurled, but he looked at both of us and calmly trotted out. Bloody cats. As he did, I niftily walked Will into their room and sat down on the bed.

"The door got stuck before," I said. "Anyway, while we're in here . . ."

I can't believe I said that. It was like when men say, "Is your dad a thief? Then how did he steal the stars in your eyes?" which someone actually used on me once, and it made me like him, because I thought there was a certain sweetness in having to choose such a hackneyed chat-up line.

Admittedly, "Anyway, while we're in here . . ." wasn't up there with the stars line, but it was still pretty cheesy. However, it worked. Will and I sat on the bed and snogged for a bit. I, for some reason, was wearing an ill-considered ruffled skirt with layers of netting, and I remember him gingerly touching the netting and then, like when someone from the gas company opens the door of the boiler and won't even get out the toolbox because the boiler's from the eighties, patting the netting good-bye and putting his hand back on the bed. I felt that the netting was the turning point, being too complicated. Did I want someone who'd be flummoxed by netting, though—who'd fall at this easy hurdle?

Either way, after that he pulled back from the kiss and said, "I'd better see if Bogey's OK. And I've got a case tomorrow."

What a perfect excuse, having a case tomorrow. I had no idea what amount of work that entailed.

Hours later, after much more booze, after Sue and Al had gone home and there were only me, Caroline, and Bobby left, we decided that Will might not have worked out that I liked him from me stealing his cat, locking it in a room, saying the inaugural line, "Anyway, while we're in here . . . ," and then snogging him, so we worked out a further way of illustrating it to him. You'd think I might have learned from the fur coat incident all those years ago, plus the fact that Will had left, but you'd be wrong. Don't forget, this was my last chance at love before my mum made me go on a date with a scientist who used to have a neck tattoo. I didn't know which was worst—the fact that it had been on his neck, the fact that it had been of Daffy Duck, or the fact that he was in five bands.

We got a small piece of paper and made a small hole in the edge of it, and then I wrote a little message to Will on the paper. We threaded a piece of string through the hole and while Caroline stroked Bogey, I tied the string around his neck in a reef knot. Not too tightly, but so it wouldn't come off. Bogey looked completely nonplussed as the note dangled from his chin alongside the bell on his collar. The idea was that he would go home, essentially delivering the message to Will, who'd then reply with a tiny note saying, "Hey, Isy! What a cool thing to do! Wanna go to Laser Quest?" or similar, and lo, a new romance would be born.

As soon as Bogey had trotted down the path, shooting us a look of disdain before moving off in the opposite direction to his house, Caroline—who's not normally a worrier—convinced herself that he would be wandering around the Dalston estate with the rope around his neck, he'd somehow get the rope caught on a hook or a hole in a fence and strangle himself, and tomorrow Will would find the corpse of his cat with a note around its neck saying, "Hi, Will! It's me, Isy!"

The next morning as we drank tea with bleary eyes, Caroline still insisting that we should be out checking all the alleyways in the area, Bogey materialized. He didn't have anything around his neck and looked really fucking pleased with himself. He even kept padding over my plate of toast and then looking at me as if to say, "Oh—*ooops*." We searched Bogey's face for signs of what had happened to the note, but he just licked his paws and stalked away from us. My phone bleeped. Mum. "He was joking about the neck tattoo! Phew!"

"You're not really going to do what your mum says, are you?" asked Caroline. I suddenly realized that of course I wasn't. I was not a child. Mum couldn't come down to London and strong-arm me to the pub, nor would she want to. I felt utterly bereft.

23

Isy discovers why there are vending machines in sexual-health clinics

All three of us had finally stopped giggling. The nurse put on her gloves slowly and carefully, and picked up the pliers.

"You'll have to keep your legs open and stay very still if we're going to stand a chance of getting this little bugger out, Isobel," she smiled.

"I've heard that before," I quipped weakly.

"Shhh," they both said, shaking their heads. James passed me four M&Ms and as I felt the cold metal touch my skin, I closed my eyes and thought of Matlock.

I'D MET James in the summer, a few months after the party where I tied the note to the cat. I had gone into hibernation from the search for The Actual Sodding One. I became solemn and self-sufficient. I stopped wearing makeup every day, and

I started to favor comfort over fashion. I took to clipping my hair back so I didn't have to dry it. I brushed my teeth while I was showering, to save time, then threw the toothbrush over the stall and picked it up when I came out. (Only once did it land in the toilet.) I didn't shave my legs or armpits much, or "do my mustache." I wore the same few outfits on rotation. I read a lot. I didn't really bother with jewelry. I listened to a lot of Joni Mitchell; and went to art museums, looked at about eight things, then spent ages in the gift shop. I saw friends a lot, and, where I could, began walking to work things and social events rather than taking the Tube, with my *A–Z* because I didn't have a map on my phone. My *A–Z* is covered in yellow highlighter and doodles, and the pages for the West End are particularly dog-eared. I considered buying a bum-bag, for ease and practicality, but I didn't go that far.

Over the months, various "artistes" who were working temporarily in London had been staying in Amy and Gav's old room. At the moment it was a Russian violinist as skinny as a rake who "played us awake" every morning. Amy and Gav now had a tiny little boy, and Sue and I were slowly making him a patchwork quilt. For weeks, five squares from my old jeans and two squares of clean hanky had lain crudely stitched together in the lounge, on top of a Woody Allen DVD and a plate with crumbs on it. I was doing OK.

I met James at a party. He had dark eyes and dark hair and big juicy earlobes. He liked running. His arms were reasonably muscle-y, but not I-go-to-the-gym-every-other-day-and-drink-drinks-called-things-like-Bulk-Demon muscle-y. He had a lovely squashy nose that was comforting to touch and that I liked to place my eyelids on when things got to be too much for me. He never took his watch off, which I liked.

"That means you'd be good to be next to in a nuclear apocalypse," I said on our first meeting.

"Why?" he asked. "Why would you care what the time was in a nuclear apocalypse?"

"It's indicative of a deeper tendency to be organized," I replied. "You'd probably have a compass, too, and some string."

"Well done for using the word *indicative* after three pints," he said.

"Cheers," I went. "That's indicative of your assumption that I haven't got long words deep in my subconscious."

Then he said, "Touché," and I said, "Flambé," and he smiled, and I smiled, and then I went into the toilets and pinched my cheeks furiously to try to make them at least pink, and bit my lips to try to make them redder and plumper, and wished to God that I'd blow-dried my hair instead of clipping it to the side with a little girl's clip with a banana on it that I'd found on the ground next to the Oval Tube station.

THE FIRST time James and I had sex, an incident occurred. The incident involved a condom, and his penis, and my vagina. There's something gloriously British, almost Adrian Mole–ish, about our approach to the condom. I imagine that in countries like Italy, men just walk round with them on all the time, so sure are they that they're only ever five meters away from a shag. But we falter a bit over here. We examine the evidence. Have we kissed and made that *mnnnm* noise? Has one of us tried, failed, and reluctantly accepted assistance in negotiating a bra or a zip? Are we now doing the kind of heavy petting that would have gotten us chucked out of a swimming pool in the eighties? Three yeses? It's C-word time. Regardless of whether you have one on you, the first words on the matter have to be, "Erm, do you have a condom?" instead of the rather presumptuous, "I've got a condom!" sung to the tune of "I'm the king of the castle!" "Do you have a condom?" is either a genuine question or, more often than not, a thinly veiled, "Are we going to have sex? I mean, I'm fine either way, it's just I put a chicken in to roast before I left and I might need to call my housemate and ask them to turn it down."

We'd stumbled back to my house, the taste of onion rings (reasonably) fresh in our mouths. As I sweatily rifled through my bag, there were some pretty second-rate utterances from me to fill time, such as, "Oooh, sex!" and the command, "Stay there!" as if it was a given that he was plotting his escape. I finally found my trusty rubber friend among hairpins and tissues, and clumsily put it on, adding buoyantly, "I'm really looking forward to this!" like I was about to eat a plate of ham and eggs. Everything was then going tickety-boo until my trusty rubber friend decided to go off piste: to come off, and wedge itself stubbornly between the upper cloisters of my vagina and the entrance to my uterus. It took a few seconds for us to realize that this had happened: it wasn't a sensation I'd ever experienced before. Once we'd dug around the sheets to confirm our suspicions, we panicked substantially. We'd realized before business had been completed, so we were OK there. But what was going to happen? Could I go into some sort of shock? Would it self-destruct after half an hour?

Luckily it was already morning, so we dressed quickly and pegged it straight to the trusty old sexual-health clinic in Camberwell. The last time I'd been there was just after I'd had the acid painted onto my wart, when I'd bumped into my ex and his upset girlfriend. What different, happier circumstances these were! When we arrived, we were giggling and hyperventilating in turn. Even though nasty and sad things go on in these places, I really like clinics and hospitals. I like the rules and the magazines and how clean they are and how if you're lucky, there's a sign in the toilets telling you how to wash your hands. James didn't feel the same about them. We sat in the waiting room and I read *Good Housekeeping*, which surely must only ever be read in waiting rooms, petrified patients gazing at some chocolate cake recipe as their mind repeatedly short-circuits toward what's going to happen imminently to their nether regions or eyes or throat.

As we waited to be seen, having been given a number to preserve anonymity, early morning morphed into midmorning, and groups of young men started to gather on the seats in the waiting room, noisily high-fiving each other, sharing crisps and Pepsi from the vending machine, and exchanging football cards. It was like a youth club where one of them might have to inconveniently pop off and have his dick looked at in a moment, but soon he'd be back to merrily pelt M&Ms at a leaflet stand. None of them talked about what they were in for. I even got the feeling that some of them were just there to hang out. They felt like I did about waiting rooms. I imagined them alone in the room with the doctor, their jubilance turned to fear now that they were away from the herd, playing with their hands as they mumbled about their symptoms, their possible shock at the doctor's request for an examination. Or were they on first-name terms with the staff? Maybe they already knew what they'd got, and it was more of a how's-your-mum-these-days and a prescription renewal. Oh, what I'd give to be a crab on the wall in one of the clinics.

When James and I finally went in, there was a smart lady doctor whose approval I immediately desired. We explained what had happened.

"He and I do know each other!" I added hastily. "We know each other's surnames and everything."

She smiled and said she'd seen it all before. Presumably she meant condoms getting stuck in passages, rather than middle-class couples bleating on about how they're not tarts. Actually, probably that, too. She produced some pliers, had a little dig, and hauled the condom out. It looked pathetic and guilty, dangling limply in the grip of the pliers, ashamed to have made the break for freedom. She asked us, po-faced, if we'd like to keep it. We said, why of course, and then we went to a café for some ham and eggs.

24

Isy refrains from feeding hamburgers to the baby

My only experience of raising a child occurred in the late nineties, when I persuaded my then musician boyfriend, Tom, to buy a Tamagotchi from London's Chinatown. Tamagotchis were pre-Internet key ring–sized toys that were supposed to create the feeling of bringing up a kid—the toy was a "baby" and you had to feed it whenever it cried and teach it stuff and change its nappy. Tom was in a band, and we were living in a studenty house in South London. There was a TV in the back garden, facing the house, which was supposed to signify that TV watches you, not the other way round. There were also loads of other abandoned stuff in the garden, like a bike, and a vacuum. They weren't watching us, they were just keeping the TV company. Looking back, bringing a child into that environment wasn't a great move, but we had high hopes. When it was old enough, it could help with the cleaning up, and one day maybe join the band. We had a slight issue understanding the instructions that came with the Tamagotchi, which consisted of seemingly unrelated pictures that looked like this:

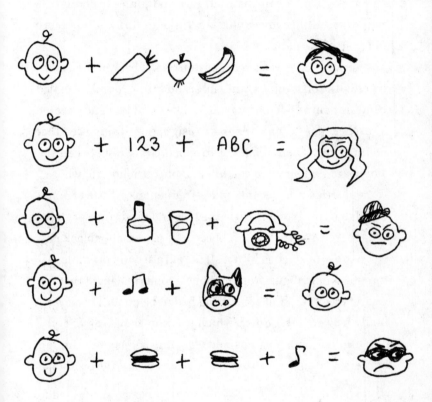

After studying the little pamphlet for a while, we worked out what to do. We called it Tarquin (ironically, of course—we weren't animals) and proceeded to feed it a hamburger whenever it cried. This went on for a few months until Tarquin became a burglar, which we knew because he was still crying but he'd started wearing a mask over his eyes and carrying a sack. I didn't know that Chinese burglars carried sacks, too, like all of ours do over here. Studying the pictures on the instructions, we could only conclude that if you feed a baby hamburgers and forget to change its nappy, it will become a burglar. I like to think it was more because of his name.

Luckily there was a reset button on the back of the Tamagotchi, like on humans, and the second time round we called him Graham and fed him fruit and he cried less and became a teacher, but he had a look of resignation in his eyes that haunted me. Then one day I dropped Graham between the sideboard and stove in the kitchen of the Soho café where I worked. His cries became more frequent as I flitted in and out of that tiny kitchen, carrying pies and mash and spaghetti Bologneses, getting told off because I was wearing black nail varnish again and had bitten all the skin around my nails. All the staff knew about Graham, but customers thought that the crying was mice, and something had to be done. Then eventually he went a bit quiet, which was somehow worse, and I dug him out with spatulas and wooden spoons, fed him ten burgers, and threw him out the window toward the brothel.

"Do you want to hold him?" said Amy. A familiar nervous wave washed down to my stomach. James and I were sitting on Amy and Gavin's sofa in Bristol, and I was looking at their baby for the first time, who was not a Tamagotchi, and who would be eating organic baby rice rather than burgers.

"*He* does!" I shouted, pointing to James, who grinned, scooped the baby up, and effortlessly ka-dunked him onto his lap.

Four months together, and James and I had slipped into the steady rhythm of coupledom. His family was very welcoming, and I felt like I'd known them forever. I'd met most of his friends, and he mine. He had walked in on Sue in the bathroom and we'd all been able to laugh about it. We'd started doing the "we" thing, the habit I had previously abhorred in other couples. "We prefer the episodes of *Seinfeld* where you don't know where the plot's going," he'd said the other night at a dinner party (more on this shortly). "Do *you*?" I'd said. "I never know where the plot's going. Nor do you. Separately from me." Then later, when we were all clustered round his friend's expensive table eating cheese off what looked to me like a common bathroom tile, I said, "We put croissants in the oven for six minutes," and I heard myself say it and I thought, *Well, it's true, but also I want to stab myself in the hand. But then I'd only have one hand, and it would be tough to spread jam onto those perfectly warm croissants.* Hmm. He had a pet name for me that I liked, and that he'd greet me with every morning. We'd done the late-night revelations thing: I'd told him the story of Simon and the package tape in one of those fragile postcoital chats where, smug from endorphins, you topple over the wrong side of the what-to-reveal-and-what-to-omit-about-sexual-history tightrope, and he'd cringed so much at Simon's use of the term *Mrs. Mimsy* that I'd stopped before the end. I didn't have a pet name for James yet, but one can't force it, as you know. I didn't want to recycle one this time.

He was a bit older than me and, for the first time in my life, I was going to dinner parties. I learned early on. Don't take a dusty bottle of Advocaat instead of wine. Ask if you should take your shoes off. (This suddenly seemed to apply in every house we went to.) If you're not directed to a seat, try to sit apart, so that you talk to other people instead of holding hands under the table and giggling. Say the food's nice within the first few mouthfuls. Attempt to surf on a wave of tipsiness rather than going under. Don't flinch when his friends call their children "mate." The children: names with silent *ph*'s and *th*'s, with extra *e*'s and *ah*'s hanging on the ends of them for dear life, other names that seemed like they could only have been scrawled on the back of a receipt by a paralytic Italian man in a pub on the way to the registry office. Oh, and was I scared of the children. Scared of dropping them, of talking to them, of not talking to them. I felt that they immediately saw my weak points and pitied me so much that they didn't even bother to capitalize on them. Like I was back at school, awkward, pudgy, clumsy, ill dressed. I longed for something to put a full stop on matters, like a poo, or a need for a certain bedtime story. Left alone with a four-year-old momentarily, I would find myself saying things like, "Do you know how an engine works? Nor do I," which would inevitably be succeeded by a thick silence and lots of staring, from both parties.

"Go on, Isy," said Gav. "Have a hold."

I couldn't put it off any longer. I cautiously moved their tiny, beautiful baby, who had a very normal name, from James's lap across to mine. His fists were balled and his eyes were screwed shut and his skin was as thin and delicate as doilies. *Please stay asleep*, I prayed. Recently a friend's kid had held up a picture he'd drawn close to my face and, while I was "admiring" it, punched his hand *through* the paper and into my cheek. Surely Amy and Gavin's baby wasn't capable of this—yet.

"Relax your shoulders!" said James.

"I bet you never thought you'd be holding our baby!" said Gav.

"Good practice!" said Amy. I nodded.

"Would you get married first if you had a baby?" Gavin asked.

"Yep," we said in unison. These days, James and I were often circling around the topic of settling down together. Each miniconversation was like we were on a golf course and always hitting the ball too far, yet getting progressively closer to the hole each time. We'd avidly discuss the fun elements: what we'd cook if we lived together, where we'd get married, who certainly wouldn't be invited to the wedding, the song for our first dance, and having quadruplets called Harry, Larry, Barry, and Gary (poor old Barry and Gary)—like when you start your school band and design the album cover before writing any songs.

Amy and Gavin's new home was pretty much how I'd imagined it would be. It was so homey, I just wanted to move in and sit between them, hugging both of them and watching shit telly like the old days, the three of us pissing ourselves laughing at tiny things only we understood. It was almost Christmas, and as well as the tree, Amy had put up homemade bunting. Rows of glittering Christmas trees and snowflakes dangled merrily, the ends of the strings taped onto the mantelpiece or wedged between Ben Folds CDs. They were living in part of a big old house, and they had two bathrooms, although one also contained a washing machine and tax returns. They'd told us with barely suppressed glee (and who can blame them?) that upstairs lived a real wizard called Justyn, who had one very long index fingernail that the baby would try to suck. His name had previously been Justin and he'd changed it to Justyn, like an amateur version of my old boss Fyl. On my own in the kitchen, I craned my neck out of their window and glimpsed a few dusty jars in their shared garden, balanced along the wall next to the flower bed, containing different-colored herbs and plants, which must belong to him. I idly pictured him trying to get into them with the short-nailed hand, tutting, and having to swap over. What functions did that long nail have in Justyn's magic? Stirring? Scooping? Pointing? Beckoning?

On Amy and Gavin's shelves, there were rows of different-sized Tupperware tubs labeled with things like:

SPAGHETTI
GAV'S SPAGHETTI
TIME [CROSSED THROUGH] THYME
FLOWERS (DRYING)
DUMMIES
BLACK PEPPERCORNS—GRIND FIRST
CLOVES
WILD GARLIC
SHOP GARLIC (IF NO WILD)
AMY BREAST PADS KEEP OUT!!

Who in God's name would be trying to steal her breast pads? Justyn? Maybe to make some lily pads for fairies? I liked the breast pad one because it reminded me of all the signs we used to have on the outsides of our bedroom doors in the eighties. The more exclamation marks, the more it dilutes the meaning of the sentence. It doesn't go full circle, the more there are, and become meaningful again. I think postcards are the only exception. You can put as many exclamation marks as you wish on postcards, because they're never truly authentic anyway: you don't write merely for the recipient; you're half writing for the postman. I once found a bundle of postcards for sale in a library, spanning different years, all from the same Sarah to the same Carol. Even though they contained a criminal number of exclamation marks, I surmised that underneath, they were good mates. From a holiday in Sussex, Sarah wrote:

> *Hi! How's Bromley? No. 42 still part of our road?*
> *Have you run many people down lately? (sorry!!) . . .*
> *We're having a nice restful (well fairly) holiday*

> *here in Selsey. The picture on t'other side is of one*
> *of the lovely Sussex villages we've visited (it's pro-*
> *nounced "Bozzum" (!)) with a very old church that*
> *has a genuine Anglo-Saxon window—wow!! (not*
> *the one shown, though, typical!) Please tell Gordon*
> *(your brother) that I haven't met Selsey Bill yet but*
> *will keep looking . . . ! (Ha, ha, not very funny!!)*

I love the fact that she puts "your brother" in brackets, as if Carol would forget who Gordon was. I can't help feeling that that bit's definitely for the postman.

When I went back through, I asked Amy about Justyn's dusty jars in the garden.

"Oh, the jars are Amy's," said Gavin. "She's growing veggies in the garden. Carrots, turnips, garlic—we should start a shop."

Amy looked a tad embarrassed. "It's only a little thing," she said. "Our neighbor gave us the seeds and stuff."

"Good for you!" I said.

"I'll get you some from the garden, if you like," said Amy. "You could grow them in London."

"OK," I said, "but I'll probably end up making them go radioactive or something."

James laughed heartily. James found me funnier than any other boyfriend I'd ever had. It was so nice. It was like I was doing gigs all the time, but really nice ones, like fund-raisers at the start of the night, or at your own wedding, which has got to be the easiest gig in the world.

Amy and I trotted into the garden so she could gather the paraphernalia for us.

"I love the fact Gav calls them veggies," I said. She linked her arm in mine.

"Just think," she said, "a year or so ago we were drinking shots and standing on roofs and shouting questions about Reykjavik to strangers, and now we're growing vegetables! And now you've got James," she continued. "I guess you two might move out of London one day, too! Move to Bristol move to Bristol! Have a baby have a baby!"

"Maybe we'll move to Bristol in about seven years," I answered. "I can't imagine leaving London."

I could sort of imagine having a baby, in the sense that I liked the idea of lolling about in caftans gobbling cake, and I would be interested to see what it would look like. But I could also see that you have to be completely sure. I was used to doing what I wanted all the time. Amy and Gavin were knackered, wired—almost like holograms of their former selves—but deliriously happy. No: blissful. Content. What was I waiting for—someone to wave a magic wand and grant me a year off work? A benevolent aunt to whisk me and a newborn away to Switzerland so I could spend months basking in mountain air, in a caftan, gobbling cake? This seemed to be a common theme.

"I'm so glad we've seen you finally," Amy said, hauling a carrot from its socket. What was I going to do with this carrot, just plant it in a plant pot? We didn't have a garden, just the roof at my house. What were we doing? "We really want to come to the cottage for New Year's," she went on, "but we just can't manage it, with the little guy's sleeping."

"Of course," I said. *Oh no!* I thought. "I understand," I said.

Little did I know at that point quite how relieved they'd be about missing it.

25

Isy discovers that trying to throw up quietly is like trying to eat marshmallows loudly

I focused on the linoleum and tried to take deep breaths. I didn't have to move for a while. The view from my position on the floor was majestic: I could see the underside of the toilet, a fossilized towel, and two of those weird little spiders that hang moronically upside down in gossamer webs; the ones that harbor ambitions to be crane flies but don't have the wings or the guts. I was jolted back to the present by a jittering of stomach cramps, and promptly shifted my head back over the toilet before it was too late. This was possibly the worst New Year's ever.

MAYBE I should explain. *No—please don't!* you're thinking. *Not if it involves throwing up! I liked the bits about penguins and* *package tape, and the condom story was a bit gross but it was over quickly—now is this really necessary?* I'm afraid to say that it is. No—I'm *proud* to say that it is. You probably shouldn't read this chapter while you're eating, but what did you expect? Put the Pop-Tarts away and toughen up! This isn't *Pippi Longstocking*— I'm a cool dude constantly getting into scrapes, and sometimes those scrapes turn bad. You can find the strength to read on. Also, there's stuff about *Take a Break* magazine.* You'll be OK. I promise. I'll be holding your hand the whole time—after I've washed it.

On December 30, a small group of us had piled into Keith and headed to St. Davids in Wales, as usual. James was joining us straight from his parents', so he would arrive on New Year's Eve separately, and as Amy and Gav weren't coming this year, it was me, Sue—who was missing her mum's birthday for the first time ever—Mark, and Al, who was still Sue's boyfriend and now very much a part of our group. I couldn't believe that it had been a year since that moment in the service station when Amy and Gav had told me the baby news. Their little boy had been born, and I had a gorgeous new boyfriend who I was soon going to introduce to our punch of many colors, locals who dressed like monks, and that Crevice Sex game I made up where you all have to lie in a row on the floor and then bang your pelvises into each other and kick each other in the backs of the legs.

---

*If you haven't had the pleasure of coming across it, *Take a Break* is a real-life magazine whose brightly colored cover is adorned with such jewels as "My husband's cross-dressing hell" and "I had sex with a ghost." There are also crosswords.

As our little group chugged down the motorway, Al announced, "Guys, I feel sick, and it's not gonna fit into my Monster Munch bag." I couldn't believe he'd managed the word *munch* even in this circumstance. Mark promptly pulled over onto the hard shoulder and made us all get out and climb onto the bank, as poor old Al hunched over his Vans and confettied the weeds.

"*Nnnnnngh*," he said as he slumped back in. "I hope I haven't got the norovirus. My dad's just had it, and we touched the remote at the same time."

The cottage was exactly the same as ever. A VHS player in pride of place, creaky old armchairs that moved with you as you shifted in your seat, and the musty air of a building that's rarely inhabited. Mark made some extra-strong G and Ts, we began a game of Twister, and we all put Al's little moment down to too many turkey sandwiches.

By nightfall, everyone but me had full-blown norovirus. There were endless cubbyholes in the cottage, and strange landings with dusty bureaus on them, and approximately seven games of Connect Four—the decrepit boxes held together with browning tape—but only one bathroom, which was an en suite attached to the downstairs bedroom that no one slept in because it was so grim but that everyone was now rushing through. While I lounged in the cozy living room that evening on a leather sofa that felt like an old friend was hugging my arse, glugging port and cutting my toenails with some rusty scissors I'd discovered under the sink, all around me was a veritable cavalcade of noro-mayhem: sprinting with pajama bottoms down, with hands over mouths, with hands

over bums; frantic pounding on the bathroom door; screams
of "Hurry up, it's coming out!" and "Do it in the kitchen sink!"
I felt a heady combination of guilt and relief as I pulled a face
that said, *Ulp!* whenever any of them happened to catch my eye
as they hurtled through the living room, each in their own
private hell, while I swirled my lovely port and got into a text
argument with my sister about whether Derbyshire or Staf-
fordshire oatcakes are better.

The next morning it was New Year's Eve, and no one was
any better. The patients lay motionless on duvets in the living room so they could be close to the bathroom. It was like
an airport when flights are delayed. I flitted around them,
Matlock's Florence Nightingale, careful not to make contact,
handing out pints of water and pressing play on the *Top Gun*
video and generally being a bit smug that I had escaped the
illness. I'd been saved by the NoroGod, because I was in love.
I called James to tell him the situation, but he insisted on still
coming, which pleased me greatly. We couldn't be apart for
our first New Year's, for God's sake! We agreed that if I hadn't
gotten ill yet, I wasn't going to, and he said it wasn't fair for
me to look after them on my own. He arrived in the late afternoon, armed with antibacterial hand gel and British spirit,
and by the evening we were all watching *Cocktail*, pausing it
every twenty minutes or so for someone to take a trip to the
loo. It wasn't exactly the New Year's Eve any of us had planned,
but I was having a better time than the previous year, when
I'd just broken up with Sam. There wouldn't be any skinny-
dipping in the sea this year—at the moment, with the others
so ill, I didn't see how we'd ever even leave the cottage.

That night, I'd been asleep a couple of hours in a Crevice Sex–type position with James—which is pretty hard in a single bunk bed—when I awoke suddenly, sat upright, thought for a split second, "Do I need a piss?" and then found hot vomit erupting out of my mouth at an alarming rate. I tore down the spiral staircase, uncontrollably spattering the ceiling, walls, baseboard, and floorboards with sick, like an evil sprinkler on the rampage, stumbled over the sleeping bodies in the living room, and, as I finally retched over the toilet, realized that the NoroGod didn't exist. Or if He did, He had played a most hideous trick on me.

In the morning everyone was starting to feel a bit better, while I was entering my own world of hell. How the tables had turned! I just wanted to sleep—I got in a bad mood if anyone tried to sing to me or make me watch *Cocktail*. It was suggested quite soon that I should perhaps dwell in the bedroom attached to the bathroom, the one that no one would sleep in, so that I could have my own space and, more important, be in quarantine. James still wasn't ill—he'd even gone for a beach run, like someone out of *Sweet Valley High*. I lay in the bed, staring at the ceiling, picturing James pounding the sand beneath his feet. How disciplined to go for a run on New Year's Day. I hadn't ever thought I'd end up with someone who ran on machines, let alone beaches, but I think you have an idea of what your "type" is, and it's often not how it turns out. He didn't use moisturizer—as far as I knew. I supposed he could do it secretly. Maybe I'd find some Nivea stashed under his bed one day. Ah, if he'd gone to that trouble to hide it, I'd forgive him. I marveled at myself in my old age, counting the Formica pattern on the ceiling from left to right and back to left again. I really loved him if I could potentially let that go. I realized in that moment that the moisturizer thing was less an actual requirement of mine and more of a stubborn clinging-on to my younger self. It could just as easily have been eating capers or spending more than forty pounds on glasses.

My temporary bedroom resembled the bedroom in *Trainspotting* that Renton is locked in when he's trying to go cold turkey off heroin, which is pretty much how I felt anyway. There were gaping holes in the floorboards, revealing spider Narnia beneath—proper spiders, not the upside-down amateurs—and I was lying on an old pilled sheet draped over a graying mattress with wayward rusty springs poking out in all directions, covered by a mustard blanket. If anyone needed the loo—they were going in the garden when they could—they'd scamper in with their hands up like latecomers to a theater, hissing, "Sorry! Can't help it! Sorry!" as they picked their way over the clothes and towels strewn on the floor. Later, James would come and leave water on a tray in the corridor outside the bedroom door, knocking softly and whispering, "Brave Isy. Thanks for this." I felt like someone from Eyam, the Derbyshire village that chose to isolate itself during the plague, thus increasing the risk to its own people but saving others. "Can I have a story?" I'd croak from behind the door, hearing distant sounds of Hungry Hungry Hippos being played and shrieks of, "Half an hour for every gram and then another half hour! Baste it in olive oil!"

The next morning I felt a bit better and thought that if I

rested enough, I should be close to normal by the evening. Then the inevitable happened: I got my period. I desperately stuffed wads of toilet paper into my pants, then dragged myself over the floorboards.

"Oy!" I shouted from behind my door. "I know you're having a great time out there with your fucking chicken, but I've got my period and I need you to get me some supplies!"

I could hear a quiet bubbling of conversation from the kitchen, so I decided to venture out. I opened the door. The waft of roast dinner hit me hard, but on I went. This wasn't Eyam. This was St. Davids. And it had a village shop. I walked forward, gathering strength. The abandoned moth was emerging from its stuffy cocoon to join the roastie-guzzling butterflies. As they jubilantly fought over a chicken wing, I materialized in the doorway with my mustard blanket draped around my shoulders. They all had hold of the wing and turned their heads in unison.

"Oh, hello, *you*!" Mark said, eyeing my greasy hair and ashen face warily. "Are you better?"

"A bit," I said. "I don't want any chicken. I need you to go to the shop for me."

To hand it to them, Mark and Al agreed to go to the village straightaway, while James would stay and tend to the roast. They rammed as much food into their mouths as they could— "for sustenance—it's a twenty-minute round-trip"—then shoved their plates into the bottom of the oven.

"Get sanitary towels, yeah? Not tampons," I said, digging in my wallet for a couple of quid. All my possessions looked really alien to me, even though I'd only been ill for a few days.

Oh, I've got a Nectar loyalty card! I thought. I started to see the light at the end of the tunnel.

When the lads had set off, I plodded back to my room and read a ten-year-old *Take a Break* I found guiltily stuffed under the mattress. I heard the back door go. The sanitary towels! There was a rustle of plastic bag, then the sound of the oven being opened.

"It's all right," I shouted. "You don't have to warm them up. I've been using them for years at room temperature."

"No, we're getting our roasts out!" Al laughed.

"Yeah!" added Mark, opening my bedroom door, a York-shire pudding in his hand. "As if we'd try to warm up sanitary towels!"

Then, with the assured confidence of the waiter whipping off the silver platter, he handed me a pack of nappies. Babies' nappies, decorated with little yellow ducks and pink bows.

"Hey! Come here, both of you!" I shouted. Mark and Al entered the corridor, wiping their hands on their jeans. "What the fuck? These aren't sanitary towels."

"They're the same, aren't they?" Al proffered before scuttling back to join Sue and his Yorkshire pudding. Mark remained, avoiding eye contact.

"Are they the same?" he said.

"Are you serious?" I spluttered. "Have you ever seen a woman's body?"

"They're made of the same stuff, though," he went. "It's like carbohydrates. If you haven't got rice to go with chili con carne, you can have bread."

I went back into the en suite and placed one of the nappies inside my pants, then stuck the sticky tabs onto my hips. I pulled my pants and jeans up. I felt better. Why didn't they put pastel pictures on sanitary towels, of women riding motorbikes and running in local elections? I went out and they plated me up a roast. I could only eat the potatoes but I managed some flat Coke, and then in the evening I had banana on toast. That night, with me on the mend, James ventured into my room. We lay under the mustard blanket, and I told him about Roy the Penguin, and that Sam had moved out of his flat and that as far as I knew Roy was still in the attic, and James told me that if I rescued Roy from Sam's attic he'd adopt him, and I started to cry, then went off to be sick for the last time, then returned and cried some more.

26

Isy discovers why you shouldn't burn teddy bears on barbecues

I'd searched painstakingly through my tatty diary to find the address, but I hadn't really needed to—as soon as I spied the peeling maroon paint on the door and the wonky silver numbers nailed to it, I felt the ghosts of butterflies in my stomach, even though I knew he'd moved out ages ago. I stood across the road, steeling myself. There were two things I had to do. This was the first, and I wanted to do it alone.

I'd rehearsed what to say: "Sorry to disturb you, but I believe there's an inanimate penguin in your attic, and if he's still here, he needs to be rehomed." I wanted it to sound kind of official, like I was from the police. I would use the passive form—"he needs to be rehomed" rather than "I'd like to rehome him"—and "I believe there's a penguin in your attic," rather than "I hope there's a penguin in your attic," or "Is there a penguin in your attic? Is there is there?" I'd inserted the word *inanimate* so I stood at least half a chance of being believed, but I hadn't expanded on it in order to try to ignite a sense of enticing mystery around Roy—he could be stuffed, or a robot, or perhaps a real penguin literally crippled with shyness.

I started toward the front door, and stopped myself. What if whoever answered thought I was a burglar? I have a checkered history regarding the definition of a burglar. At nursery school, we were asked to draw a picture of what our dads did for a living. Not our mums, because this was the eighties, and women didn't work then, of course—apart from once a month, in the bedroom, after watching *Family Fortunes*.

This is what I drew:

The teacher said, "What's this?"

I replied, "Well, my dad's a burglar, and every night after my mum's gone to bed he takes me out burgling with him. And I'm not allowed to go in yet, but I sit in the back of the car and he locks me in so I'm safe, and I keep guard, and he tells me tips, like, 'If you hear a noise, don't be scared, just carry on,' and 'Always carry a sausage in case there's a dog.'" I went on. "I've got a whistle I have to blow if I see someone coming. Once a fat woman was walking down the road while he was burgling her house. I blew the whistle three times, and he ran out the back of the house just in time with thirty thousand pounds' worth of jewels and a Scrabble set."

My teacher knelt down beside me and spoke softly. "Very good, Isobel," she said. "You've been very good," and she gave me a gold star and then she called my parents in and sat them down and said, "Are you a burglar, Dr. Suttie?"

No, surely I didn't look like a burglar. Whoever answered would see that. They'd smile and let me in, and I'd go up the stairs, past the square patch of wall that was slightly lighter, where Sam's calendar used to be, and a bit farther along, an incredibly faint, thrice-painted-over line of Magic Marker in the shape of a woman. This had occurred when we'd gotten hammered one night and I'd flattened myself against the wall and said, "Draw round me like I'm a body in a crime scene, but a vertical one because we're in space and there's no gravity," and, amazingly, he had. Ten seconds earlier the walls had been cream, and then there was the wobbly outline of me in Magic Marker, just like that.

He'd insisted we paint over it a few weeks later when it was clear that it was a bit of an eyesore. The atmosphere was the opposite of one of those paint adverts where a young couple, he floppy haired and puppyishly inept, she the only woman over twenty-five who seems to be able to pull off dungarees and pigtails, are roller-painting their new, airy house. In the advert version she flicks paint on his nose, he laughs, the next scene she's pregnant. With me and Sam, the first and second coats of paint caused the marker to fade but stubbornly peep through from underneath, like when Lady Macbeth's trying to wash the blood off her hands, or when Adrian Mole paints over the Noddy wallpaper in his bedroom with black paint but you can still see the bells on Noddy's hat, or when people try to change their accents in the first week of university. After the third coat, you could only see it if you knew. However, I was careful not to stand in exactly the same position against the wall now, in case when I moved away it looked like I'd left a sort of dirty gray aura. I did once meet a therapist who told me my aura was the color of "cement," so it would have fitted, at least.

Whoever answered would give me a ladder and I'd go up to the attic, wondering if Roy would be there. Could there be a whole zoo of papier-mâché animals that Sam's other exes had made him—monkeys and giraffes and elephants, all just hanging out? Maybe that had been his thing—taking girls to the London Zoo and talking about how cute animals were, just to see if they'd bite the bait. There's always stuff in attics that looks initially useful but turns out not to be, like broken toy electric guitars and SodaStreams from the eighties, and loads of that yellow fluffy stuff, and this one would probably be no exception. Whenever I move in any-where with an attic, I go straight in to see if there's any-thing left over. And if I found a penguin in my attic, it'd be brilliant. I'd clean the dust off this penguin I'd found, and put him in the lounge, and fill his stomach with books and dried flowers, and everyone who came round would think I was insane, like when people find a dog in a pub and it could maul anyone at any time—they'd say I didn't know where this penguin had been, who'd made it and why, whether it contained asbestos or needed to be exorcised.

Of course I didn't go in. I didn't really want to know what had happened to him. He probably wouldn't be there, and even if he was, how would he fit into my life now? I took one last look at the house, and closed the book on Roy. As the bus went back toward Camberwell, I didn't even look out the window.

When we got back, it was on to item two. I instructed Sue to go onto the balcony and light the barbecue. This was (a) because I had no idea how to light a barbecue and didn't in-tend to find out at this late stage in life, and (b) because I was climbing onto the desk in my bedroom in order to retrieve the memory box that Sam had brought round when we'd broken up. It was right at the top of the wardrobe, where Amy and I had placed it more than a year ago.

I was so determined to get the box down quickly that I couldn't be bothered to clear everything off my desk, and the box was a lot heavier than I'd remembered, so as I brought it down off the top of the wardrobe, my knees buckled beneath me. I was too high off the floor to jump down, so I was forced to slowly but surely sit on my laptop, which was on my desk. I heard a clear, drawn-out crack, but I couldn't move from my position because of the weight of the box—I shouted for Sue, and she rushed in holding some fire lighters. She took the box off me like it was a feather and shoved it onto the bed, and I gingerly got off the laptop. When I opened it, it looked fine, and I convinced myself it could be OK. Maybe the crack had come from my knees. When I turned the computer on, however, the screen had the appearance of a puddle with gasoline in it—all different colors that swirled about hallucinogenically when you pressed on it. Great.

I knew I was going to have to fork out for a new screen, so I became even more determined to do what I wanted to do with the box, which I was now refusing to call a memory box, as it made me feel like I was in a Richard Curtis film. Sue had gotten the barbecue going, and we laid all the stuff out beside it. Al was there, and our friend Kobs, who was staying, and the four of us took the stuff out of the box and laid it on the patio. Things Sam had given me that had ended up at his, and random stuff from our time together that had completely escaped my mind. There were copies of *Eats, Shoots & Leaves* by Lynne Truss, *Timebends* by Arthur Miller, and *The Book of Bunny Suicides*; loads of photos; a Richard Pryor video; eight CDs, including *Matters of the Heart* by Tracy Chapman and Queen's *A Day at the Races*; a weird camisole-cum-negligee with guitar picks dancing on it; a napkin with the results of a Shithead card game written out on it from a train journey; a sugar cube from a hotel; a windup ET; some maracas; a dark green scarf with dried red pesto still on it; a blue penguin eraser from the London Zoo he'd bought me on the day we'd met the real Roy;

and a teddy bear with a bell tied around its neck from Spain. That was the crop of our time together.

Sue wanted to cook some meat first to test the barbecue, but I threw *Eats, Shoots & Leaves* onto the grill, and it went up quickly enough. Kobs got some oil and vinegar from the kitchen—"For religious purposes," he said solemnly. "We're not making a salad dressing"—and we doused all the contents of the box and they told me to say a prayer. I didn't know what to say, so I said, "Dear God, please take these gifts as a sacrifice and do what you will with them. I don't think you'll want the dancing-guitar-pick negligee any more than I did, but maybe you can use it to wrap a baby angel in or whatever. Thanks. Take care. See you around. Amen."

I was quite used to praying. When I was a kid, I'd say the Lord's Prayer, then grace, then I'd add, "Please bless all the soft toys," as I had a shelf of soft toys in my room. After about a year of doing this, I realized with horror that I'd been neglecting all the hard toys—rubber ducks and so on—and thus the addendum became, "Please bless all the soft toys and hard toys." About a year later, I thought about all the soft and hard *live* animals I'd been neglecting—chicks and hippos and so on—and my guilt was mind-boggling. My mum reassured me that they hadn't been dying because of my failure to pray for them, it was because of foxes and hunters, and also that my forgetting to say "please" in the prayer a couple of times when my cousin was staying over hadn't made a difference to the soft and hard toys I *had* been including. That was when I moved on to the Ouija boards.

One by one, the items went onto the barbecue. It broke my

heart to burn *Timebends* and the Richard Pryor video, but I just wanted everything gone. Last was the teddy bear, right on top. Everything else had burned to cinders, but this teddy just would not burn. Its stuffing was so tough that though the outside crackled away, the flames wouldn't take to its insides—they were just smoldering. We watched as slowly it melted itself indelibly onto the grill of the barbecue, like Jesus on the cross, the bell around its neck blackening but remaining completely intact. And then it just wouldn't move. We all tried for ages to scrape it off, but, like the vague outline of me on the wall of Sam's old flat, the teddy's outline remained. So I had to buy our landlord a new barbecue. If I added to this the price of replacing my computer screen, all in all it had cost me £185 to get rid of the memories of Sam—£5 more than it took to make Roy. Yet I just didn't care. Sam might have thought he had the last laugh, but I had a brilliant boyfriend with whom I was about to go have a Mega M&M and Movie Sausage and Mash Marathon; and Sam was probably going out with a skinny girl who went to pottery cafés and wore shoes with faces on the toes and didn't ever laugh for more than three seconds.

27

Isy decides that it's cruel to keep a goldfish in a T-shirt

James and I decided to move in together. I was surprised when people said, "It's a bit early!" which everyone did.

"It's a bit early!" said Sue and Al, as the three of us jostled for the middle seat at the pub quiz. "It's a bit early," my mum sighed, as she prepared to decline her friend from bell ringing's invitation for me to meet her newly divorced son. "It's a bit early!" went the newsagent downstairs as I bought an ice cream. "Aren't you going to make him a papier-mâché animal first?"

"It's a bit early," Amy said on the phone.

"Why does everyone keep saying this?" I protested. "You're the ones who were so desperate for me to find The Actual One."

"What do you mean?" she replied. "Hang on, sorry. No! Stop eating hair off the floor! Oh God, he's covered in sweet potato and he's rolling in hair on the floor."

"I didn't know Gavin could roll," I said, smiling. She didn't hear me. A few minutes went by with various noises of cajoling, pleading, and whimpering, while I bit the skin around my fingernails, then picked up a hand mirror and studied the bags under my eyes. She came back to the phone.

"Sorry, Gavin's got him now. Go on."

"Look, it just feels right to move in together," I said.

It did. We were constantly staying at each other's houses, to the point where all our housemates had said we should just do it, if only so they could have the time in the bathroom they required. We had mastered the tricky art of having sex quietly, which had been funny at first but now was a bit tiresome. In my flat, Sue and whichever actor was staying in the spare room that week and I were used to just meandering into each other's rooms when we felt like it, sometimes without many clothes on, to discuss a pressing issue or just lie down and have a moan. This wasn't ideal now, even though I missed it. None of this had been an issue with Sam because we'd seen each other far less.

It was an easy decision to move in with James—his housemate was moving out, so there would be a gap. Also, his flat was cleaner than mine and he had a kitchen trash bin with a lid. It was settled. I was about to go skiing, and then I'd move in.

"Well, good for you," said Amy. "Anyway, he's got to be better than some of your other housemates."

She did have a point. I've lived with lots of housemates who at first seemed to be "delightfully eccentric" but were rapidly revealed, once the contracts were signed, to be "virtually impossible to live with." There were some I ended up loving, like Manchester-born Claire-with-an-*i*. She had a massive gap between her two front teeth, so big that she once bit into a jam doughnut and a perfect arc of jam spurted through the gap, went about two feet in the air, and landed on a VHS copy of *Basic Instinct*. She said things like, "Me and men are like chalk and cheese. If chalk and cheese have sex in a closet at work." She worked in an old people's home. Once when I was going on a first date, she said, "I've got three rules and three rules only with dating, Isy. Rule one: always go to a brightly lit area on the first date. Rule two: never kiss on the first date. Rule three: always use a condom on the first date." There was also Rachel the Australian, who spoke terribly slowly and with a great lisp, who used to float around in green tops and brown trousers, saying things like, "Do I look like a tree?" and "Who's Ben Nevis?"*

But the most eccentric housemates I've ever lived with materialized in my second year of drama school, the year of the package tape and the fur coats and sneakers on multi-lane roads. I'd left it too late to find people to live with, so I ended up in a small house on the outskirts of Guildford with other students from my course: a Slovenian, a Hungarian, and a Frenchie (a Frenchman, not the pink-haired one from the film *Grease*, which would have been beyond my wildest dreams). As there were four people and only three bedrooms, I slept in the living room for two terms, on a bed that tripled as a sofa and a dumping ground for ashtrays, goulash, and

---

*Ben Nevis is famous for being the highest mountain in the British Isles. Although it's a possibility that there are also men called Ben Nevis, who are sick of people asking if they have their heads in the clouds.

late-night, wine-fueled theories about the inner mechanics of Brecht. My being awake was not a requirement for these chats. My mother kindly sewed me a cover out of our family's Scottish tartan to drape over my bed in the day. I never washed it, and it immediately became a fossil of our filthy existence—our own collective tartan, which was the color beige. However, I soldiered on. I had a roof over my head and I'd learned the difference between prosciutto and pancetta, and maybe living with fellow Europeans would mean that one day I'd be able to expand my accent repertoire.

Anja, the Slovenian, always dressed in black, or black and purple. She once told me that she'd only wear clothes whose colors could be displayed in a bruise. She was not renowned for her subtlety and had been sacked by the clothing outlet Gap for telling a woman—who hadn't even asked—that her bum was—not looked—big. I felt that my sunny attitude cut through all this—she brought some grit out in me that I hadn't previously known I had, and I hoped that, in return, the spring in my step would lighten her deathly plod. The only outdoor space near our house was a massive cemetery, which we would frequent on summer evenings. One night she cupped my chin roughly as if she was going to kiss me (later in the year we did start to kiss each other in bars, for ten seconds only, in return for a pint of Stella "each—not to share"), studied my face solemnly, and said, "You are different to others. You have . . . *European soul*." What did this mean? I knew I liked the idea of having a European soul. Surely it meant I was sensitive and cultured and had an innate understanding of baby-foot, the table-football game.

"Cheers, An," I said, biting the arm off a Jelly Baby, wondering if that was the kind of thing people with European souls did.

She continued, her eyes scrutinizing me. "Your face . . . it's like your eyes are from one face . . ." I tilted my chin up into the lights of the cars, letting her see more, all the better to continue with her poetry. "Your nose from another . . . and your mouth from yet another." She paused. "Together? It does not make sense."

That August, I went to stay with Anja in Slovenia. I went for a couple of weeks to a country whose language I knew not a word of, and came back knowing the words to a song about a Slovenian man with a small penis. On the way there, the airline mistakenly sent my suitcase to Italy, so for the four days until it was delivered to Anja's house I had to wear her clothes—all she gave me was a sleeveless T-shirt and very short shorts, which I duly wore around the town, my legs the color of two furious lobsters within an hour. During this trip I did what I often do when I'm on holiday—but even more so, as I would sit for hours not understanding a word of what was going on around me. I planned out lots of different hairdos and types of clothes I was going to unleash on the world when I got back to the UK, including braiding all my hair, sewing a belt from rainbow-colored pom-poms, and making a T-shirt with a plastic "window" that would contain some water and an unfortunate goldfish. I spent the whole of a bus journey to Ljubljana imagining a small valve at the bottom of the T-shirt that would allow you to release fish food into the window without losing any water, or the iridescent captive within.

I quickly grew to understand that in Slovenia, women go topless on the beach. "Actually, it is disrespectful not to," Anja informed me as we trekked onto the sand, tiny brown women swarming everywhere. I hardly ever go swimming. In my suitcase, which was still winging its merry way to me, I had my only swimwear—a maternity swimsuit I'd acquired from my friend's mum at a holiday resort years ago when I'd forgotten mine. It was very old, and its elasticity had been stretched to the max. The sides were gray and threadbare and, due to its incredible stretchiness, as soon as I had been submerged for even thirty seconds, it would gather water in great amounts in the chest and crotch areas, so that when I exited the sea or pool I had breasts a foot long that tapered into points, and an upside-down-witch's-hat-shaped "penis" that reached down to my knees and swung violently from side to side as I walked.

"Because your suitcase is not here yet, I have bikini bottom for you," Anja said.

Sod it, I thought. *This is what life's about! So what if my body is so white, it's reflective? I've got a European soul!*

So I got behind a rock and scrambled out of my shorts-and-sleeveless-T-shirt combo and into the bikini bottom, my heart genuinely pumping in my chest (there's something so brilliantly un-British about nudity that I sometimes wonder how we reproduce), and then lay sunbathing on my front for an hour before putting my clothes back on. I'd done it—I'd passed a test. When we got home that evening, my suitcase had been delivered. I've never been so glad to see Marks & Spencer underpants in my life. Anja watched me take off the crumpled outfit of hers I'd been wearing for the last few days, then announced, "Everyone in my town say you are prostitute."

"Why?" I answered, alarmed.

"Because you wear tight top and hot pants in the town. It is fine to show your breasts on beach, but you should not wear skimpy clothes on street. This is religious village."

"Why didn't you say anything before?" I garbled, glad of my jeans, which were already rubbing against my sunburn in greeting.

She paused. "I could not think of English word for *prostitute*."

Frigyes the Hungarian was a different beast altogether. He could hardly speak any English, but one of the few things he could say was "VAT." He was obsessed with VAT. Every other sentence was, "What is it, VAT?" Despite his name sounding like "fridges," he carried all his food, and I don't mean a few slices of bread and ham, I mean *all* his food—so a loaf of bread, goulash, a large hunk of cheese, peppers, tins—and for that matter all his cutlery (not just one set) around with him in an increasingly dog-eared Sainsbury's bag. Sometimes he'd set off for college ahead of us and we'd see a radish or a slice of salami on the pavement and know the route he'd taken, just like the hen night with the pink feather boas in the Walkabout Plymouth.

None of us ever ventured into Frigyes's bedroom, but in the third term it was decided that he and I would swap rooms so that I could have a few weeks of listening to David Gray's *White Ladder* in solitary confinement. I had my own bedroom! It didn't matter that it was the tiniest bedroom I've ever been in, and had a single bed. My new bedroom had a sink, which I could wee in if I put one foot on the windowsill and the other on my bedside table; and a door, which meant I could wee in my sink to my heart's delight. You had to stand on the bed in order to open or close the door. Living in there was like being in a never-ending episode of *The Crystal Maze*, which, as I'm sure you can guess, I adored.

"WELL, YOU certainly won't be pissing in the sink in your new bedroom," chuckled James, stirring slightly too much milk into my tea. Strictly speaking, it wasn't a new bedroom I would be moving into—it was James's room, in his flat. I felt very excited and nervous about moving in. On the one hand, I supposed it would be like a never-ending sleepover, and on the other, I knew it wouldn't—I would be moving all my worldly possessions in. Well, apart from the Isy and Jo's Dating Agency stamped certificates and the Joey McIntyre poster with the hole in the mouth, but you know what I mean. There wouldn't be just my emergency Rimmel eye shadow and stubby concealer, which currently dwelt on the sink, on a little island among his razors and hair clay. (Luckily I had no preexisting rules about hair clay.) There would be my guitars and computer and receipts and hair-removal cream and loads of odd sheets and pillowcases I'd picked up over the years.

I really was growing up. I'd lived with a few blokes I'd ended up banging, like with one of my first acting jobs, when I played the fairy godmother in a tour of *Cinderella* up north in venues that were not necessarily suited to pantomime, and shacked up with the actor who played one of the ugly stepsisters in a house where eight actors were cozily sardined into three bedrooms, but that was different. It wasn't just me and him in that house, for a start. And you don't go shopping for sofas together when it's you and an ugly stepsister. You don't have the ugly stepsister's in-laws over. You don't make up songs together, and you certainly don't put croissants in the oven for six minutes. Ugly stepsisters don't even eat croissants. They abhor them. It's simple with an ugly stepsister. You go for a curry with your ugly stepsister, the other ugly stepsister, Cinderella, and Buttons—who's always dropping Fulham Football Club references into the script, risking the ire of the audience—hurriedly blow the ugly stepsister, then share a bowl of midnight cereal before getting up at five in the morning to go perform at a school, then a caravan park, then Wigan Bingo Hall, to people who try to play bingo at the same time, realize that can't happen, get angry, reluctantly watch the show, then say, "Not bad, actually. You lot should do acting properly."

I looked about. James's flat was bright, if a little modern. Take his tables, for instance. I like old, weary tables scorched with endless Venn diagrams of coffee rings; tables with chunks gouged out of them from years of absentminded scratching and fevered banging of fists and heavy pots dropped, the wood marbled with valleys of packed-in butter and potatoes and port. Tables the equivalent of Moe from *The Simpsons*. James's tables didn't have a single dent, and they were decked out with matching coasters of Tube stations. I was sitting on a sofa with a throw on it. I'd never lived in a house with throws before. If a spill won't come out with a bowl of hot water and dishwashing liquid, it's meant to be, in my book.

Speaking of which, he had a big book collection, which I was looking forward to diving into. We were working out what we would have double copies of now. *Catch-22*, *The Catcher in the Rye*, *Cold Comfort Farm*—all the classic *C*s. We'd decided to reread them at the same time, but I suspected he was a quicker reader than me and conversations would contain spoilers, especially as I hadn't actually read *The Catcher in the Rye*.

"Here you go," he said, handing me the too-milky tea. I put the mug down and began to scan the back of *The Catcher in the Rye*. Maybe I could just read the Cliffs Notes. "Coaster!" came the cry from across the room. There was going to be a bit of adjusting yet. Then he put on *Curb Your Enthusiasm*, the most classic of all the *C*s, and I put the book on the floor and placed my closed eyelid on the tip of his nose.

28

Isy finds that you don't need to know more than one verse of "The Lonely Goatherd" from *The Sound of Music*

I like to say I go skiing every year. In reality, it's more like every three. I went for the first time when I was about ten, in Bulgaria with my family, and adored it, although my dad got bitten on the thigh by a local stray dog with rabies and had to be transported to the hospital in what I recall as a wooden ambulance. The ambulance men knew the dog by name and shook their heads smilingly when they arrived, as if the dog was their wayward mate Kev who'd been caught scrapping again. The only two things I took away from that holiday were a love of skiing and the memory of being in the back of the wooden ambulance, looking down through the gaps in the wooden slats at the road whizzing past below, while my dad sat there with his leg up, still in his ski suit.

I say "ski suit"—my ever-thrifty mother had decided that

our family would probably only ever go skiing once and that it would be a waste of money to buy ski suits for us, but instead of trying to borrow them, she opted for the easy option of converting seventies duvets into ski suits. First she applied waterproof spray, and when it had dried, she laid each duvet on the floor. Big brown-and-orange flowers, pink-and-orange diamonds, mustard-and-light-blue stripes. We lay on top of them like Christmas angels with our arms at right angles to our bodies and she drew round, made us shuffle along so we were on a new bit of duvet, drew round us again, and then sewed the two bits together with a zip down the front. The front and back of mine were made of matching fabric and the same went for my sister, but because of a mistake when she was cutting out his outline, the front of my dad's ski suit was made out of a different duvet from the back, which was the only thing that could be worse than having a ski suit made out of a duvet. When the four of us were skiing together, we looked like the Bay City Rollers on a break from tour, crashing over the crest of the hill.

I'm not a great skier, but what I lack in technique I make up for in bravado and denial. My motto is, "If I think I can do it, I can do it." That's all very well for persuading yourself to finish that bit of work or to force yourself to do the dishes (although I find that even with my motto I often can't manage that), but when you're at the top of a black run that's mostly ice with bits of grass showing at the sides, or a run that's dotted with thousands of moguls (the humpy bits of snow that you have to sort of part your skis to get over), it sometimes doesn't wash.

This year I was in a big group, as usual, in a great, no-frills resort with my mates Caroline and Bobby, various other mates, and a few people I didn't know but would soon get to know over breathless après-ski conversations about spectacular wipeouts and arguments with ski-lift attendants and that moment you nearly knocked over a class of beginner skiers who were following their instructor in a perfect line like a domino run begging to happen. On the first morning, I decided to have a two-hour lesson with an instructor. To cut costs, I shared the lesson with another girl in our group called Jane, who was a horseback rider and very practical and much better than me at skiing. Every time I fell over and took ages to get up, they'd both get more exasperated. I decided to try to make things better by showing off my A Level French.

In the evening, while the others had their pudding in the chalet, I walked to the pay phone in the center of the resort and called James. I told him about my lesson, omitting the "I am hot" part, and he told me to be careful on the slopes. That's what everyone says when you're going skiing—like when you're doing a show and people say, "Break a leg!" They don't really mean it, unless you're a method actor playing Richard III.

Later in the week, I had to take a trip to the little cluster of shops with Caroline and Hannah, our other best mate from school, because Hannah had developed thrush, which is quite common when you're skiing because you're wearing lots of layers close to your body. No biggie. The only thing was, none of us knew the French word for *thrush*.

"It's OK!" I crowed as we swung open the door to the chemist. "I'll be able to tell them." This was my chance to make amends for the "Je suis chaud" incident.

"Bon matin, monsieur," I said brightly, striding toward the man in the white coat, who said nothing, just placed both of his hands onto the counter and sighed expectantly. "Je voudrais"—then I pointed toward Hannah's nether regions with a conspiratorial look—"le oiseau." He looked completely blank. So did Caroline and Hannah.

"What does *oiseau* mean?" hissed Caroline, who hadn't done French.

"Bird." I smiled. "Don't worry, he must have misheard."

I repeated to the man: "Nous voudrons"—I leaned in—"le oiseau, s'il vous plaît."

By this time a few people had gathered behind us in a queue, which told me they must be British.

"Je ne comprends pas," said the chemist, throwing his hands up.

"Le oiseau!" I proclaimed, pointing again to Hannah's crotch. "Itchy itchy! *Non dormir!* Cannot sleep!"

"Oh," said the man behind me, obviously a seasoned skier from the look of him and his expensive skis. "She's got thrush."

"Oh!" said the chemist, reaching behind him for a white tube of cream. "If only you'd said."

Straight after that, we were up on the slopes, and I was determined to use what I'd learned in my lesson the previous day. The resort we were at, Val d'Isère, houses the men's black run from the 1992 Winter Olympics, and it's still very much up and running. It's called La Face. Hannah said no way—the morning's events had been quite enough for her—so I was with just Caroline and Bobby, who are both skilled snowboarders, and I am a mediocre skier with delusions of grandeur, and that's an unlikely combination. Most people stick to their own, but we three were like when two lions encounter a goat and you think it'll end in carnage but they become the best of friends and go around everywhere together. They're faster than me, but they always know when I've fallen because they hear me screaming, "Désolé! Désolé!" at whoever I've bumped into, or whoever's bumped into me, because in the heat of the moment I can't rule out that it isn't my fault, and they patiently gather themselves at the side of the run and wait for me to catch up.

On the ski lift up to La Face, Caroline told me in hushed tones—Bobby was on the lift behind us—that the two of them were probably going to try for a baby after the holiday, but she wasn't telling anyone else because if you do, people keep asking you if you're pregnant, as breezily as they might ask if you're going on holiday. Apparently this happened to her friend after she'd gotten married, until she eventually went on holiday out of frustration and ended up getting pregnant. I squeezed her hand.

"There's only two or three days a month you can get pregnant, you see," she said. What?! I'd thought there were two or three days a month you *couldn't*!

"Do you reckon you and James will have kids?" she said. I realized that this was the new question, now that we were moving in together. People were also asking if we were going to get married, of course.

"I hope so," I said. "Not for ages, though. Why do people keep asking if we're going to get married? It's the same as you not wanting to tell people you're trying in case they keep asking you and you feel inadequate. I don't remember people being this obsessed with the future when we were twenty-two. We just used to get pissed, didn't we? Who gave a shit whether we were going to have steak or cornflakes for dinner the next day? I feel like no one lives in the present anymore."

"Mmm," she said. She didn't really know what to say when I said stuff like this. She'd done business studies at university. We gazed at the animals' paw prints in the snow below us as we got toward the top. I saw that I'd had a text from James saying that he'd e-mailed me a link to an auction we should go to next month so we could choose some new stuff for the flat together, asking me to look before the end of the week and let him know what I liked.

Off the lift, we began La Face, flying past a few big, brightly colored signs that said, CAUTION! EXPERIENCED SKI-ERS/BOARDERS ONLY! Then we got to the steep bit of the run. I started cautiously. I was going slowly, but who cared? I was living in the present! I was doing La Face! Or rather, La Face was doing me. I was going too slowly. I turned twice, then fell onto my front right in the center of the run, gave up trying to stop, and proceeded down it like Superman. When I finally landed at the bottom, I found myself within a circle of people of various nationalities and ages, all applauding and pissing themselves laughing.

"Phew!" I said as people moved off, shaking their heads in an ominous way. "I can't believe I've done La Face! Let's go for a brandy and I can look at this auction site."

Caroline and Bobby looked at me. "Isy, that wasn't La Face," Caroline said. "It was just the slope that leads onto La Face."

I looked down, and now that the crowd had dispersed I could see that before me was the steepest run I'd ever seen. It was clearly visible from the ski lift, but I'd been too busy ranting about not living in the present and looking at wolves' paw prints. What good was all that to me now? No wonder there had been the massive yellow signs. There was no way back, or to the side. The only way down was down La Face, and La Face, let me tell you, was not smiling.

In front of me was a 2,905-meter sheet of mostly black ice set vertically into the mountain, with a drop of 972 meters and grass coming through at the edges, because there hadn't been much snow for a few days, and also because of course it's not hard enough to ski on vertical black ice—why not throw in some shrubbery for good measure?

"Do you want us to call the emergency guys?" said Bobby. "They can take you down on a stretcher."

That sounded nice. Maybe there would be hot chocolate and a DVD player on the stretcher, too.

"No!" said Caroline. "You wanted to live in the present, didn't you? Well, this is it."

They sped off. I gritted my teeth and did the same, thinking of it as something I was going to traverse, not go *down*. The French ski instructor had told me the previous day that I should loudly sing whenever I was scared, as it would help me to focus. Despite the fact that I love music and write songs, the only song I could think of was "The Lonely Goatherd" from *The Sound of Music*. My heart beating ten to the dozen, I began to sing at the top of my voice, higher than normal because of my fear, "High on a hill was a lonely goatherd, lay ee odl lay ee odl lay hee hoo!" My intention, because I knew none of the other lyrics, was to repeat this on a loop.

I didn't need to. I fell almost immediately, then started to hurtle down at about triple the speed of the previous slope. I desperately tried again and again to get the edges of my skis into the ice, but to no avail. All I could do was try to stop the snow from blinding me as I flew down, screaming, "*Désolé! Désolé!* Move! Move!" When I was able to angle my head to look downward, I could see no end to the run. People seemed to part as I reached them, a hair's breadth away from being completely wiped out by the screeching girl in the bright pink ski jacket. My speed meant that snow was packing itself into my mouth, eyes, nose, hair, neck. I tried closing my eyes, but that was worse. I tried curling into the fetal position and opening myself out again—but nothing could stop me. People on the ski lift above me gaped in disbelief. I thought, *Maybe I'm dead, and this is purgatory, and I will never reach the end.* I let my body go limp. There was no point in fighting this.

Suddenly Bobby was standing in my path on his board, about twenty meters ahead of me.

"No! No!" I screamed. "I'll wipe you out! I'll kill you!"

"You won't!" he shouted. "You can stop!" I don't know how it happened, but I managed to get the edges of my skis in at the last moment and came to an abrupt standstill millimeters before his board. I could barely see for snow and tears. My face was red raw. I unzipped my ski jacket. There was snow packed inside it in every single crevice, which had rushed in under my chin as I'd bolted down.

"Come on," he said, "you're more than halfway down."

I shakily got up and got my poles in order and tried to set off again, but it was too much. I just sat on my bum and side-slid my way down the rest of the run, with Caroline coaching me from the side. I didn't care what people thought anymore. Anyway, surely this held more dignity than singing "The Lonely Goatherd."

MUCH LATER that night, Bobby and I were walking to our chalet with Bobby's cousin Joel. It was about two a.m. and we had drunk, in order: beer, vodka, a blue spirit from a dusty bottle, a green spirit from a dusty bottle. Everyone else had gone to bed ages ago. As we staggered past the main ski run that led into our resort, we saw a load of tables piled up outside a restaurant. In a few moments, a plan was hatched. Maybe it was just because we were hammered, or maybe it was because I felt like the snow had conquered me that day and I wanted to show it who was boss. Together, we stole one of the tables and began to carry it up the hill. It had a shiny top, probably vinyl, and wasn't very heavy at all. We got really high up on the run. Then we turned the table over so that the shiny top was against the soft snow, which was utterly pure and untouched because the snowplows had already been round getting it ready for the next morning, and the table legs were sticking straight up, like a dead insect. Then we sat on it, in a line, with me jammed in the middle and each of them holding on to an upside-down table leg.

Silent with concentration, we pawed at the snow around us with our hands to get going. We expected to shunt along for a few meters, then grind to a halt. But it turns out that when you put a shiny table onto snow, the snow really bloody likes it, and we immediately started speeding down at about sixty miles an hour, spinning around and around at the same time. Bobby and Joel commando-rolled off the table onto the run on either side, but since I'd been in the middle, I couldn't get to the edges of the table to do the same. I just had to cling on to the legs for dear life, hysterically laughing. After what felt like an eternity, I landed in the net fence at the bottom of the slope, with such force that it took about ten minutes for the three of us to untangle me. When we got back to the chalet, Bobby and Joel took Joel's suitcase back to the same run and went down it on that, but I had to turn in, in case my good luck was about to run out. As I stumbled into bed, I realized I'd never replied to James's text about the auction. "Sounds good! xx," I put. I decided not to tell him about La Face or La Table—he'd only worry.

The next morning I woke up with one of the worst hangovers ever, but because Bobby and Joel had one, too, it didn't seem as bad. At breakfast it transpired, to much jollity, that a guy in our group had ended up having sex with one of the chalet girls in the sauna when everyone had gotten back. He had red stripes emblazoned on the backs of his legs where he'd been sitting on the sauna bench while they were doing it, which is better evidence than any hickey.

29

Isy discovers why the
NHS really is better

As the nurse sobbed into my hair, I let my head relax on her heaving bosom. I'd been in there for twenty minutes, and I hadn't even had the bloody Pap smear yet.

I was an old pro at Pap smears. About eight years previously I'd had an abnormal result and had had to have further tests, where they paint iodine in you and put a camera up there while you look at a postcard of Paris taped to the ceiling, sneak a look at the screen, and then hastily return to looking at Paris for the rest of the procedure. I'd been given the all clear, but I had to have smears every year for a bit, and so I was pretty on top of when they were. I knew the procedure inside out. The preamble; the undressing behind the curtain; the cold telescope thing going in; the breezy chat about the weather or local roadwork or past smears; then the tickly, alien feeling of the stick scraping the sample off.

This time, when my name got called by the doctors' reception desk—my surname causing havoc, as usual—and I went into the small room, there was a large West African nurse sitting behind a desk. She looked extremely weary—beyond the end of her tether. She looked like her tether had been stolen from right under her nose and she didn't even care where it had gone. Whenever I see anyone in discomfort, my instinct is to blast them with jollity. They're a red rag to a relentlessly chirpy bull.

"Isobel," she sighed, looking at her notes, "when was your last smear?"

"February 18 last year," I gabbled, slightly too loudly, as if I was waiting for my gold star. "Almost exactly a year ago."

She looked up slowly and smiled. "Ha! No one ever knows when their last smear was."

I told her about the colposcopy and the yellowing postcard of Paris I'd looked at during it. She didn't seem uninterested, but it wasn't like she wanted to know more. I told her more. "It was the Eiffel Tower," I said, "on a drizzly day. There weren't many people around, but I guess they just had to get the photo done. I quite admire them for not photoshopping in sunshine and tourists."

She smiled and rubbed her face.

"You look a bit tired," I said, which was a slight risk, but I was on a roll. I was doing my usual of trying to put off the inevitable with chat.

She blew her nose. "I am tired," she said. "My son broke every window in every house on the street last night. He is totally off the rails. I don't know what to do."

"Wow," I said. "Every window? Even the frosted bathroom ones? They're quite thick. That's almost admirable."

She ignored me. "And my beautiful daughter is skipping school," she muttered. I thought she was going to add more. Had her beautiful daughter broken every traffic post on the street? Every heart?

"I'm sorry," I said. I was in deep. These kinds of problems couldn't be met with a chummy pat on the back, or a Kahlúa and milk.

"Why do you think she's skipping school?" I asked.

"Her dad is not around," said the nurse, hauling herself out of her chair, pulling a blue curtain across the bed, and moving to the outer side of it. "Come on. In there. Bottoms off."

To preserve dignity and so you don't feel like you're in a niche porn film, you should always wear a skirt for smears. I always forget to wear a skirt to smears. Behind the curtain I pulled off my trousers, knickers, and shoes but left my socks on, as if they would provide some sort of modesty. "Ah, she saw my vulva, but not my ankles!" I had on a short T-shirt, so I was completely naked from the waist down. Then I heard a snuffling sound, and I realized that the nurse was softly crying. I'd never been in a situation like this. She was a fully clothed health professional. I was a supposed woman, half naked. I didn't even know her name. I went for the generic approach.

"Oh, don't worry," I said gently through the curtain. "It'll be OK in the long run." Would it? How could I know? Her son might go on to break every window in every house in Britain.

"You are kind," she spluttered. "But it won't. Oh, come here!"

I didn't understand what she wanted me to do, so I popped just my head around the curtain like a villain in a pantomime, a villain wearing no trousers or pants. And I saw that she was holding out her arms, weeping. Of course I ran to her, and we hugged. My cheek sank onto her buxom chest, which was hiccupping with sobs, and I repeated, "Don't worry. Don't worry." If anyone had opened the door, this is what they would have seen:

After a few minutes she calmed herself and told me that we must be running late now but we still had to do the smear. We both traipsed behind the blue curtain, and I lay down on the bed as she started to get out the instruments.

"Do you have a boyfriend?" she said as she bustled about at the end of the bed.

"Yeah," I said. "He's great. I'm really, really happy. We're going to an auction next week cause we've just moved in together, to get some stuff."

It turned out that living together *was* a bit like a never-ending sleepover. We could do things that took longer, hardly aware that time was passing, because there wasn't the pressure of me having to go home. We'd sit cross-legged on the floor and watch the washing machine go round and round, or spend ages making Thai chicken curry from scratch. He made me packed lunches and put little notes in them. We had already been on a few holidays where we rented cottages that used to be chapels or farm sheds from people called things like Malc and Jilly, and we'd research the real ales and the walks before we went. I'd even started to like walks, as long as they led to a pub. I'd discovered that he always liked sleeping on the same side of the bed, no matter where we were, and got grumpy if that side of the bed was up against a wall, leaving nowhere for him to put his book and glass of water. In those instances, we'd swap the pillows to the other end of the bed and lie the opposite way round so that "his" side became free. We'd sit together in the cottages that used to be chapels, gobbling local ham and ginger cake, and I'd gaze out at the fields and write a load of material about a field from a cow's point of view, which was swiftly scrapped upon my return to London. I was becoming more confident with his mates' kids, and was now even considering going to an auction. Everything was perfect. I felt so sorry for the nurse. Her life was so stressful, and she still had to come to work and be civil and accurate.

"Have you ever been to an auction?" I asked the nurse. She laughed and shook her head. I did what I often do when I'm having a "procedure"—I talk incessantly to cover up what's really going on. It's the opposite of a haircut, where the hair is at the forefront and the chat drifts in and out of the picture. With a "procedure," I make the chat the aim, with the medical stuff sneakily taking place in the background. I also attempt to reassure myself that I'm the bravest patient they've ever had by asking the person carrying it out if they've ever had any real wusses.

"Oh, yes," she said. "Of course. The other week, one woman said the Lord's Prayer throughout."

"I tried to have a smear test when I was on my period once," I said, "and the nurse said no." How did that make me brave?

"They were correct to say no," she said.

She put the metal thing down and leaned on the bed.

"Once," she said, "I traveled back to Africa to see some of my family, after I'd been living in the UK for a long time. I was used to the cold here and I was wearing lots of clothes. On the plane, I suddenly got my period and I didn't have anything with me. My period was as heavy as iron, as heavy as iron. And it soaked through all my clothes except for my big coat. When

I got to my destination, it was boiling hot. Everyone was in shorts. And all my family laughed and said, 'Take your coat off! You're not in England now!' and I couldn't, because my clothes were covered in blood. And I had to keep my big coat on. I was dripping with sweat. My coat was as heavy as iron, as heavy as iron. Since then, just to be safe, I've never been on another airplane." I looked at her. She cackled. "No. I always carry sanitary pads."

We both laughed.

"That's a good story," I said. "It's good to be prepared. If James and I argue, one of us sometimes sleeps in the spare room, and I like doing it because Brian Blessed's autobiography's in there, which his old housemate left behind, and I keep it under the pillow just because it's nice to read when I'm not in my own room. It's really good, actually. If anything, I'm glad when we argue so I can read it. Brian Blessed met Picasso!"

She put her head on one side and frowned, scrutinizing my face. I grinned. "You don't look to me like the kind of girl who's at home at an auction," she said. Then she sighed and put the metal thing in and I stopped talking and looked up, and this time there was no postcard of Paris.

30

The second explanation

Oh, come on—give me some credit. Of course we broke up. How rapidly and feverishly an innocuous comment about Brian Blessed can trigger the unraveling of the whole sodding tapestry.

This is how it happened. My friend Mhairi has always told me that when you're unsure about a decision, you should take out a photo of yourself as a child, smiling. Look at it closely, and ask yourself if you want that cheeky little girl to grow up and be with the guy in question, or be in the job in question, or go on holiday with that racist. Whatever. I can't tell you how many times this simple thing has helped me immediately see the light, whether I want to or not. I haven't got many photos of myself as a kid, as my mum believes in "looking forward" and also because none of my family can operate a camera efficiently, but the night of the smear, I dug around while James was out and I found my favorite. It's of me and my sister. She's about two and I'm about six, and we're holding hands. We're not dressed that differently from how I'd been in the smear—we're in tees and underpants, holding hands and grinning at the camera. But the thing that makes me love this photo is that we are covered, from head to toe, in spaghetti Bolognese.

I gazed at my sparkling eyes and lopsided grin. As soon as I was honest with myself for the first time, the result was complete and clear. If I carried on with him, I'd always be just about OK, I calculated. I'd survive for a long time, coasting on innate chutzpah. I often like the challenge of "making the best of it." But this was potentially keeping myself in a situation that I knew, and I suspect he knew, wasn't completely right. I can't begin to try to analyze the complexities of why it wasn't quite right, and I also think I owe it to him not to try. We were like a Rubik's Cube with one faulty panel—a turquoise one that shouldn't be there—so that we could never be solved, and never be calm. Any relationship or friendship is open, of course—is, and should be, always ebbing and flowing—but ideally upon a steady foundation. We were on shaky ground. But how tempting to stay together! Watching the washing machine go round, swapping the pillows to the other end of the bed, knowing what each other's silences mean! There's a danger when you've got bags of optimism, that it can spill over into denial in the right circumstances. If we didn't act now, we'd be further entwined the more time went on. Kids, marriage, buying somewhere—it had all been talked about. I didn't want it to get to the rotten point—you know: "Tonight, let's make a sauce from scratch with vine tomatoes! And later,

I will touch your flaccid penis as we both bravely gulp back the tears!"

If only it were just the making of the decision. But that's merely the start. It's the telling them, it's the tears from both of you, it's the discussions that you know are futile but must be diligently carried out, the strange dance of it all; it's the realizing that you won't see his family ever again, apart from maybe on the Tube, where you'll scuttle away and bury your face in your book, your heart hammering. There's only fire and ice in hindsight—at the time it's just a bloody miserable, never-ending business. You don't need to know how we had "the chat" (on my only free night during an acting job) or how we both cried (a lot) or about the logistical pickle of me arranging to come back and get the bulk of my belongings at a time when he was out (thank God he'd alphabetized our books and DVDs) or how each of my friends rallied round in a way I'll never forget (I was even able to move back into my old room in the flat with Sue)—you probably have similar stories yourself. It's never like in the films, is it? In the same way that deaths in films never feature the surreal, spiky reality, nor do breakups, which are a living kind of death.

My relationship with James both started and ended with a medical professional inserting a metal implement into my vagina, but the second time we didn't go for ham and eggs.

31

The last time Isy sees Ben

I spotted the underside of the hook first, and I couldn't work out what it was at all.

It was painted white, the same color as the wall, with a few bits of silver metal showing through where the paint had worn off or never been applied, and was easily camouflaged. I'd never noticed this hook before. Could it be to do with the curtain ties? No, there were no ties or anything, you just drew them. There was no equivalent hook on the other side of the window. What could it be used for? Not a picture; it was too low. Who'd put it up? How had I never noticed it? I'd lived in and out of this room for years. I reached up and touched it. It was less cold than I'd expected. I hooked my index finger round it. It felt nice. Then I remembered I was having sex with Ben the Australian.

"Uhhhmmm," I said unconvincingly, like in porn when

you know they're thinking about the fact that they're going to have waffles for dinner or they're willing the other one to finish up because they've got to collect their kid from school. "Uhhh."

Ben looked down at me. "You like that?" he said.

"Yeah," I whispered. "It's the best position after loads of food, isn't it?"

His skin smelled of baked beans, all over. We hadn't eaten baked beans. I looked up again at my friend the hook. My finger was still curled around it.

I looked up from my hook and at Ben, because he'd made a noise like when a kid falls over into mud and starts crying, then stops themselves—a kind of "Aaanghuhhhhmmm." He pulled out.

"Hey," he said, "who'd win a fight between a snake with no tail and a lion fused to a skateboard?"

I smiled. He'd made it so easy for me. I was truly alone, just like he was, and I bloody loved it. I hooked my finger firmly around the hook again.

"Which one?" Ben pressed. "Snake without a tail or lion fused to the skateboard?"

I thought hard. "The lion," I grinned, "if the skateboard was remote controlled and another lion was controlling it. An evil lion."

"That's it, babe!" Ben said. He laughed, and I did, too.

"Thank you for everything," I said. I could have kissed him.

32

Isy considers patenting Crevice Sex

All Crevices present?" I shouted. "Crevice Amy!"

"Present!" came the shout back from Amy.

"Crevice Gavin!"

"Present!" from Gavin.

"Crevice Mark!"

"Present!" boomed Mark's voice.

"Crevice Sue!" I shouted.

"Present!" came Sue's deep voice.

"Then let the crevicing commence!"

We thrashed about on the cottage floor, clutching the rug and hysterically laughing, till Amy and Gav's baby started crying. I clambered off the floor and picked him up and trotted into the kitchen with him.

"This is where your dad cooks roasts every New Year's," I told him. I took him upstairs to the dormitory bedroom, and we looked out the window at the sea and the cliffs. "That walk leads to the pub where me and your mum and dad met the monk."

We went back down the spiral staircase and into the spare bedroom. "And that's where I lay with James when I had the norovirus a year ago," I said. "When he vowed to adopt Roy." The baby smiled and grabbed my eyeball, and I yelped and giggled and we headed back into the living room.

That night, I sat on the stone bench in the freezing cold garden with Amy, drinking G and Ts with chunks of ice cream in them because we didn't have any ice cubes. The baby was asleep and Mark and Gavin were cooking a roast, even though it was nearly eleven. We listened to the waves.

"I fucking hate the sea," I breathed.

"God, I'm so happy to be drinking properly again," she said. "You can't drink much when you're breast-feeding. You just feel guilty the whole time. About everything. You know, 'Am I doing an OK job? Are they alive?' That's all you think." She took a sip. "And I felt like I was being such a dick, just wrapped up in myself and the baby, but I couldn't help it for a while."

"I didn't think about you thinking you were a dick," I said. "I thought you thought *I* was a dick."

"I didn't think anything about you," she said. "Sorry! I mean, I know you're a total dick, all the time, but I didn't think you were any bigger a dick than usual. I just didn't think about your level of dickness."

"I thought you were slightly more of a dick than usual," I said, "for a bit. Sorry. I don't now. Is it worse to think someone's a bigger dick, or not think about whether they're a dick at all?"

We watched as Moomoo trotted out onto the lawn, toward the path that led to the sea.

"I don't know who told you that Actual One thing," I said, "but it's bullshit."

She smiled at me. "I made it up as I went along to cheer you up about breaking up with Sam. What do I know?"

I put my head on her shoulder and listened to the waves. "You know what?" I said. "My New Year's resolution is to abide the sea. To get to the point where it's like that dodgy cousin you can see once a year."

THE NEXT day we walked to the same bit of beach where, two years before, I'd angrily dumped all my clothes and run into the sea. The baby was fascinated by the sand. We found a packet of toilet paper rolls in a cove—I didn't want to think about why they were there—and we sat and tried to make a fire by just putting them all in a pyramid and lighting the bottom one with a lighter. It failed. We laughed as Moomoo manically jolted around with one in his mouth, the paper streaming behind him as he frightened seagulls. Then Amy shouted, "Oy!" and I turned round and saw that she was butt naked, and I grinned and took my clothes off, too, and we ran together into the utterly freezing sea.

Of course she didn't. That's the ending that would happen in the film version. We just got a bit cold, packed our stuff up, linked arms, went back to the cottage, drank some G and Ts, and ate another roast.

Acknowledgments

First, thanks to all the people who appeared in this book, especially Amy, Gavin, Hannah, Caroline, and Bobby, none of whom asked to read it before it was published (oh ye of maximum faith).

Thanks to Josie Long and Sian Harries, who read the first draft, and to JB Morrison, Tom Bacon, and Jane Watkins.

Thanks to my literary agent, Robert Kirby, who is calm and wise to the nth degree, and to Olivia Homan and all at United Agents. Thanks to my editor, Bea Hemming, who has consistently been encouraging, intuitive, and understandably firm when I wrote in early drafts "no ending for chapter—don't worry, Bea: profound thing happens in cartoon."

Thanks to Idil Sukan for taking the cover photo and figuring out how to balance the skateboard on a bath towel so I didn't repeatedly skate into all her equipment. Thanks to the computer game Ms. Pac-Man for providing brain freefall breaks throughout the whole writing process, and to the music I listened to repeatedly: Angelique Kidjo, Erasure, Rufus Wainwright, Melt Yourself Down, Joel Bird, and the Smiths. Thanks to Upper Norwood Library for providing such a good place to write.

Thanks to all at Orion, thanks to Amanda Emery, and a big thank-you to my mum, my sister, and Geoff. Thanks to Dan for being so grown-up about not appearing in the book. You just weren't crucial enough, buddy.

Most of all, thanks to Elis and Beti Mair. I couldn't have done it without you.

A few names and details were changed, because I wanted it to be like you were listening to me tipsily gabbling about my life over a pint, and the only way I could be honest about my feelings at certain points was to change a few elements to protect people's identities.

The section about the condom getting stuck was first published in the *Observer Magazine*.

ABOUT THE AUTHOR

Isy Suttie is a comedian, actress, and writer who started performing stand-up in 2002. She has written for *The Guardian*, *The Observer*, and *Glamour* and is a regular writer and performer on BBC Radio 4, where her show *Pearl and Dave* won a Sony Gold Award. Her TV acting credits include Dobby in *Peep Show* and Esther in *Shameless*, and she has been nominated for three British Comedy Awards.